LOVING NATHAN

Loving Nathan

Searching for God's Love in the Midst of Heartbreak

MARY FOULGER

Loving Nathan: Searching for God's Love in the Midst of Heartbreak
Published by Mary Foulger

ISBN 978-1-7775007-0-2
Copyright © 2018 Mary Foulger

All rights reserved. Except for brief excerpts for review purposes, no part of this book may be reproduced or used in any form or media without permission from the publisher.

Any websites, books or other references recommended throughout this work are offered as a resource to you. These are not intended in any way to imply an endorsement on the part of the author or publisher. The information in this book was correct at the time it was published.

Scripture quotations are taken from the Holy Bible, New International Version®, NIV®. Copyright ©1973, 1978, 1984, 2011 by Biblica, Inc.™ Used by permission of Zondervan. All rights reserved worldwide. www.zondervan.com The "NIV" and "New International Version" are trademarks registered in the United States Patent and Trademark Office by Biblica, Inc.™

CONTENTS

	Introduction	ix
1	Does God love me?	1
2	Back to the beginning	11
3	Nathan's blessing	19
4	How does God love me?	27
5	Young family years	31
6	Life in Amsterdam	43
7	Canada	57
8	The teenage years	61
9	Finding employment is easy, right?	73
10	Nathan's last chapter	81
11	It's over	87
12	Darkness	91
13	Hannah	103
	Epilogue	113
	Appendix: Reflections on Heaven & Hell	119

INTRODUCTION

It was two in the morning when our doorbell rang on that fateful day at the beginning of May in the year 2000. My husband Mike and I were sound asleep, and the house was encased in darkness. Our eldest daughter, Abigail, had gone to Toronto to see her boyfriend, and as I stirred I assumed she had just returned without her door key. In hindsight this was silly, since she had taken Mike's car, and he kept the house key on the same ring as the car key. But no one thinks very clearly when awoken from sleep at two in the morning.

It was pleasantly warm, and I saw no need to bother with a dressing gown since it would only be Abigail at the door. My cute, Snoopy nightgown may have been a little short, but it was not revealing in any way if someone happened to be passing as I opened the door. I pulled myself from the bed, feeling a little annoyed that I was the one getting up and not Mike, and descended the stairs to our front door. I was putting together some words of complaint, ready to unleash on my daughter when I opened the door, but when I peered into the dark, it was not her standing there at all but two police officers. My mouth must have dropped open just slightly as one of the officers quickly addressed me and asked me to confirm that I was Mary Elizabeth Foulger. He then wanted to know if I had anyone else at home with me. I said that my husband was asleep upstairs and the policeman asked me to bring him downstairs. I gestured them into the front room and went up to get Mike. I was now more than a little scared. What was going on?

"There are a couple of policemen downstairs and they want to talk to us both," I said to Mike, prodding him to wake up. Abigail had been driving on a really busy highway and my first thought was that she had been involved in an accident. It would have to be a really bad accident for there to be two policemen knocking at our door. Fear was beginning to overwhelm me.

The policemen didn't leave us guessing for long. As soon as Mike and I were back downstairs they asked us, *"Are you the parents of Nathan David Foulger?"*
We nodded. Nathan was our son, though he had left home just over six months previously. "We are sorry to inform you that Nathan drowned in Victoria, British Columbia, some time in the last couple of days."

It had to have been a mistake. It was someone else, and they just thought it was Nathan. It could not be my son because God was looking after him. I was a Christian, I trusted God, and I had prayed for him hour after hour after hour since he left home. It *had* to be a mistake. Some other poor mother had to go through this, not me. I was a woman of faith. I had been confident that if Nathan was ever in desperate need then God would have alerted me to pray for him. I would have been obedient and prayed and God would have saved him. That was how things worked. Yes, this was surely all some terrible mistake.

The policeman was still talking, giving us the details. Nathan had been living out west, and a few days previously he had gone camping with a couple of friends. Late one evening he appeared to be upset over something and had decided to go out walking by himself. His friends became concerned when he failed to return after some hours and they went out looking for him. There was no sign of him. It was dark and they were too anxious themselves to venture far from where they had camped. Thinking that perhaps he had made his way back to Victoria, where they all lived, they tried calling mutual friends. No one had seen or heard from Nathan. Early the next morning they contacted the police. The police began a search and a day later, eight miles downstream from where he and his friends had set up camp, they found Nathan's body. The police said that they had not felt it necessary to inform us of Nathan being reported missing but obviously now they were giving us the whole story. At two in the morning on May 6th, 2000.

It made no sense to me. Nathan knew how to swim. He was strong and healthy. How could he drown? The policeman elaborated. He said that the water was moving very fast, and it was cold also. The snow was melting in the mountains and was adding more water to the river. He told us that Nathan would not have struggled for long, which I know was intended to be comforting, but it didn't help. Since that conversation I have played the last 10 minutes of Nathan's life over and over in my mind.

Heavy Doc Martin boots pulling him down, tied half way up his calf so he could not quickly kick them off.

Cold water crashing over him as he desperately tried to grab at a tree by the side of the river.

The twig he grabbed quickly breaking away from the tree, and Nathan not being able to pull himself out of the river.

Heavy wet clothes pulling him under.

Probably praying, crying out to God to save him. Perhaps also crying out to God to forgive him.

And what was God's response? God let him drown.

Once the officer had relayed everything pertinent he asked if there was anyone he could call for us.
Whom do you call when your world has fallen apart?
They left a message for our pastor. Then they offered their condolences and took their leave. I felt sorry for them. The second officer was quite young and he hadn't said a word. He was clearly finding this visit very difficult.
I had pointed out some pictures of Nathan we had hanging on our walls. I did not cry in front of them. I held my emotions in check while they were there. In fact, I held my emotions in check for quite a while after they left too. Initially I just felt numb. This was not really happening to me. Perhaps it was just a bad dream. This was the sort of thing that happened to other people, not to me.
Mike and I just sat there, together in the living room. Each of us alone in our thoughts. Both of us devastated. A few tears came, but not many. We held onto each other for a while and then we just sat once more. Silent. Not sure what our next move should be. Where was God? Did he care? How could he care and just let Nathan drown? Our son. Our only son. No, it could not be true. God was not that cruel.
Abigail arrived home around four in the morning. She was happy, having had a great time with her boyfriend. She was rather surprised, of course, to see both her parents sitting in the front room when she came

through the door. We quickly let her know the tragic news. Nathan and Abigail's relationship had become strained over the last few years. Nathan was no longer kind to her and he rarely seemed capable of seeing situations from his sister's perspective. She no longer felt close to him and it had been a relief for her when he moved away. She received the news with little emotion and went upstairs to bed. I was surprised at how easily Abigail seemed able to go to sleep. Sleep was no longer an option for Mike or myself.

After another couple of hours of just sitting in silence, our pastor, Ed, arrived. It was kind of him to come. He had known Nathan and some of the struggles that he had faced in his short life. Ed also knew that things had not always been peaceful between Mike and I, and our son. Despite the many disagreements between us, Ed knew that we were totally committed to our son and that his death was the worst thing that could have happened to us. What could anyone say at a time like that? Ed was very wise and he did not say much at all. He prayed a short prayer, expressed his sympathy, and then simply sat in silence alongside us. As much as I appreciated his visit, especially the fact that he did not offer a bunch of empty platitudes, I was in a hurry for him to leave. The pressure was building and I was ready to shout and rant and scream and I did not want to do so in front of my pastor.

Eventually Mike and I we were alone again, just as the day was beginning to come alive outside. As we had sat there in silence I had tried to pray. My relationship with the Lord was strong and the natural thing to do was to turn to him for help. I wanted to hear him speak into my heart but was afraid at what he would say. *"Sorry, I wasn't paying attention,"* crossed my mind.

And where was Nathan going to spend eternity?

No matter what he had been doing in the last few months he had once loved the Lord. When he left home he was very angry with the church; like so many others before him he felt hurt and let down by God's people. He never stopped believing in God though. The truth was, he had experienced too much of God to not believe in him. He just wasn't following him anymore, wasn't making any effort to please him. As I sat there, anxiously wondering if my son would be accepted into heaven or not, I somehow sensed him crying. It was not a terror kind of cry and I in no way felt that Nathan was being turned away. It felt like a cry of anguish; despair that he had not shared the love of God with his friends in Victoria, particularly with his girlfriend.

Our youngest daughter woke up not too long after Ed left and we didn't waste any time keeping the sad news from her. Hannah was only ten and thought the world of her brother, even though she hadn't seen him for several months. She was immediately distraught. *"How could God let this happen?"* she asked. We had no answers and were quietly asking the same questions.

A dream died in my heart that night and a nightmare replaced it. I had prayed, hoped, and believed that Nathan would come home no longer bitter or angry. The first few months after he left I wasn't sure what God was saying about the situation but eventually I felt the Lord tell me that within the next three years Nathan would return to us. Now I felt totally let down. By God, specifically. He had failed me—in the biggest possible way. I had believed that God was going to change Nathan, heal him, help him overcome his problems, and that he would return to us as a man walking with the Lord. I had been so confident that I had even shared the promise I felt I had received from God with our church one Sunday morning. Coming home in a coffin really did not cut it.

Now we would have to begin our lives again without Nathan and without any hope of ever receiving him back.

Loving Nathan

CHAPTER 1: DOES GOD LOVE ME?

Most people assume that when someone close to them dies, they will grieve for a while and then get over it. I certainly assumed as much. The truth is, you do not ever get over losing someone, you just gradually grow accustomed to the fact that they are no longer with you. I learned one of the best ways of explaining it in one of the many books about grief that I read in the months after Nathan's death. The author said it was like wearing a heavy chain around your neck. At first it feels so heavy that you struggle to do even the most basic things, like eating and going to the washroom. Slowly you begin to get used to the chain and are able to return to a more normal existence, working, cleaning, talking to family and friends, and going back to church. Over time you realise that occasionally you even forget that the chain is there, although there are always many things around you that quickly remind you. As the years pass the chain continues to be there but you have become used to it and most of the time you forget its presence.

The torment of the first few months after Nathan's death was horrendous. I would frequently dream about him, these dream often ending with his death, though most of the time it wasn't by drowning. As I struggled to wake out of each nightmare I would be very confused. I would recognise that Nathan did not die in the way I had dreamed, which meant the dream was a lie. And if the dream was a lie then that meant Nathan was alive! Eventually I would come fully awake and quickly remember that Nathan was in fact, really dead. The grief would sweep over me once again, trying to engulf me in self-pity and depression, and keep me from functioning as a healthy adult.

Well-meaning friends would try to encourage me that God still loved me, but I felt like laughing at them. One person lent me a beautiful picture book about the story of a man walking along the beach with Jesus. The man looked back at their footprints and noticed that there were times when instead of the two sets of prints there was just one. The man asked Jesus why this was, as the man assumed Jesus had abandoned him during his most difficult times. Jesus replied that those were the times when he carried the man because he was finding it difficult to walk himself. It's a popular allegory and maybe it has brought you comfort before. As for me, it just made me angry. I remembered when Abigail was very young, she would often turn to her father when she became tired and beg him to carry her. When he finally gave in and picked her up to place her on his shoulders she was always so happy. No longer too tired, she would stay in his arms anyway, happily being carried by her daddy. The whole point of being carried was to make it easier. Well if Jesus was carrying me it certainly did not feel like it. I longed for the pain to go away, I longed to feel carried. When you are picked up by your daddy the pain of walking immediately goes away, doesn't it? The pain of losing my son seemed to lessen incredibly slowly as the months passed.

If anyone who I felt close to during that early time of mourning had asked me if I felt that God loved me, I would probably have answered in the negative. I kept going to church, I kept praying every day and I kept reading my Bible. I never stopped believing that God was my only hope of salvation, I just questioned his love for me. I had experienced too much of God to walk away from him but I certainly was not worshipping him during those months. Mostly I swore at him, and about him. I knew that he was strong enough to save my son and yet for some reason he hadn't done it. How could I help but be angry at him?

It is easier for me to answer the question theologically. Yes, God certainly loves every one of us. There are plenty of scripture verses in the Bible that describe God's love for us. There are several Psalms in particular that speak of God's love, which actually kind of annoyed me during my time of mourning. I could identify with David's anger at God but not with the positive declarations that he frequently ended his prayers with. Psalm 44 has verses I could concur with: *"Awake, Lord! Why do you sleep? Rouse yourself! Do not reject us forever. Why do you hide your face and forget our misery and oppression?"* (Verses 23-24.) Did God sleep while Nathan drowned? It seemed to me that he did. The Psalmist continues: *"Rise up and help us; rescue us because of your unfailing love."* (Verse 26.) That was the positive declaration and I struggled with it. Although the Psalmist may still have been in dire straights awaiting an immediate expression of God's love, he still declares that God's love is unfailing. I simply felt like God had failed me.

There seem to be a lot more Scriptures about God's love in the New Testament than in the Old. For example, the verse that all Evangelical Christians learn before any others, the famous John 3:16, *"For God so loved the world that he gave his one and only Son, that whoever believes in him shall not perish but have eternal life."* The Scriptures are definite on this, God loves the world. Somehow I have to concede that I am a part of that and despite the pain, I too read that God loves me.

The big question then for me is, how? How does God love me? If he is interested in me individually, if he wants to be my friend and comforter and have a real relationship with me then I need to see something happen. I need to feel his presence, especially when I am hurting. Before Nathan's death I might have used the trite saying *"If God feels a million miles away, guess who moved?"* After losing Nathan, that phrase is simply annoying to me. If I am in mourning, I need to be able to raise my hand just a little and quickly feel God rushing to my side to take hold of me. In a normal relationship, when one person is struggling the other person needs to step forward and offer more love and care. My father died when I was 21 and while several friends withdrew, not knowing what to say or do, one friend simply came and sat with me for hours without saying anything. Her presence meant the most to me at that time. I wanted God to do the same, to simply come and be with me. Yet for months after Nathan's death I felt nothing of God's presence. Did he love me? I suppose he did but I wondered why I couldn't feel it.

Another trite thing we Christians tend to say is that prayer should be a conversation, not a monologue. But what happens when God is silent? During that time the reality of my prayer sessions was that I was the one doing all the talking. Or yelling. Or crying. And God would say very little in response. Oh, I would read Scripture every day too and often something from what I read would speak to me. But it felt like God would say one small thing and then I would talk for an hour. I would pray, worship, thank God for things, ask him to help me and help others.

And then that was it. I had no idea whether my prayers were pleasing to God. I felt like they should have been because I tried to pray in accordance to what the Scripture seemed to suggest. The problem was that I felt like my prayers for Nathan hadn't been answered, which undermined my faith in any prayers being answered. I had prayed many hours for him, day after day, week after week, month after month. I prayed extensively and faithfully for my son. If anyone had earned it, I thought it was me. In the end, those prayers weren't answered in any way that I expected them to be answered. I had prayed that he would come to know that God loved him, that he would find a good job, and that he would find good Christian friends who would support him. I prayed that he would come to understand that his family was for him and not against him. I prayed that he would accept how God had made him, and that he would choose to turn his heart back to the One who loved him more than any other. Maybe Nathan cried out to the Lord just before he died, but even if he did, none of my other prayers were answered this side of eternity.

And it's not like I wasn't listening to God, or didn't have practice hearing his voice. I had a good track record, so to speak, of hearing clearly what the Lord was saying. Many times in my life I have received thoughts from God for people that when I shared them, were spot on. Such as when I felt God tell me about how a young man I met had been badly teased by an older sister when he was a young boy. Or when I felt that I should tell a young lady that she would have a ministry that took her around the world. Several years later she joined Mercy Ships, who take medical help, construction help and health education to countries that struggle to support their own people. That is why I was confident that I was actually hearing from God when I shared publicly with my home church about Nathan coming home. I did not think the promise was for Nathan to come home in a coffin. Either I was wrong, God was wrong, or something in the plan had changed. Whichever it was, I felt awful.

Clearly God did not answer my prayers for Nathan the way I hoped. Did that mean God did not love me? I would never have admitted it out loud quite like that, but in reality, that is exactly how I felt. My husband loves me, he tells me that he loves me, and he demonstrates it too. In small ways, like bringing me a cup of tea in bed in the mornings; or by giving me his last prawn (shrimp, for my North American friends) because he knows that I love them. In bigger ways, too, like sitting with me for hours in the hospital when I had an asthma attack. I am confident that if it were necessary, Mike would sacrifice part of his body, or all of it, for me. Certainly, if I were sick he would do whatever he could to help me feel better. And yet my heavenly Father has the power to change water into wine, heal someone born blind, repair limbs that have never worked before, and even raise up people who have died. He supposedly loves me more than Mike does, and also has more capabilities to reach me with that love. Yet when I have a gastric infection and I ask God to heal me, I have never experienced instant relief. Although God may help me through it, he has never responded in the way I cried out to him for— *"Please help me to feel better right now!"* Does that mean that he doesn't love me very much?

I have sometimes wondered if it took Jesus by surprise when he felt that his Father had deserted him on the cross. *"My God, my God, why have you forsaken me?"* (Matthew 27:46.) I realise that he is quoting from Psalm 22:1, but I find it hard to believe that Jesus suddenly thought to himself that now was the time to quote scripture. I believe Jesus *felt* that his father had forsaken him, just as we often feel that God is not with us. I put emphasis on felt since it could have been that Jesus felt so alone at that moment, struggling with the physical pain plus the mental anguish, that it only *seemed* that the Father was not there with him, when he really was. Isn't that a very human experience? Maybe at that time Jesus was questioning whether the Father truly loved him. It could be that God did turn away because Jesus was carrying the sin of the world, but I think Jesus was demonstrating that he was human, just like you and I.

The truth is that being loved by God does not mean that everything will always be easy. We only have to look at the book of Job to see that. Things started off going really well for Job, until God seemed to mess it up for him by boasting to Satan about his servant. *"Then the Lord said to Satan, "Have you considered my servant Job? There is no one on earth like him; he is blameless and upright, a man who fears God and shuns evil.""* (Job 1:8.) Satan is not impressed and suggests that Job is only such a great guy because of how much God has blessed him. God then allows Satan to do whatever he wanted with all of Job's possessions and family. It is interesting to note that Job clearly believes that God was the one in control of everything, so God was the one who took his family from him. Yet from our perspective we can see that Satan was the one who causes disasters to fall on Job's livestock and children. Job's response to all the loss in his life is well known, *"Naked I came from my mother's womb, and naked I will depart. The Lord gave and the Lord has taken away; may the name of the Lord be praised."* (Job 1:20.) Job did not accuse God of doing anything wrong, so we are informed by Scripture.

After Job's refusal to sin against God, God once

again boasts to Satan about his servant. This time Satan is confident that if Job was to get sick then he would curse God. God gives Satan the freedom to move again although he is not permitted to actually kill Job. Now Satan afflicts Job with painful sores from the soles of his feet to the crown of his head. Poor Job has lost his wealth, his children, and now his health. And he does not know that all this is happening because God is proud of him!

Job's friends were not very encouraging. Although the three of them spent the first seven days just sitting with Job, unable to say anything because of the enormity of Job's suffering, they blew it on day eight. Their theology was awful, the stuff of trite sayings and rehearsed wisdom. They were convinced that if Job were suffering it must be because he had some sin in his life. Yet they were wrong. It is certainly true that sin does cause us to suffer, so if adversity strikes us there is nothing foolish about asking the Lord if there is sin in our lives that might have precipitated the adversity. If nothing comes to mind though then we should not live in condemnation. Job's friends, however, were not willing to let go of this theme—not that they had any idea what it was that Job had specifically done wrong. Unfortunately there are many who believe and behave similarly in the church today.

I find it incredulous that 'friends' would say to someone who has just lost his wealth, his children and his health *"Blessed is the one whom God corrects; so do not despise the discipline of the Almighty."* (Job 5.17.) What kind of God are they following? A God who disciplines by killing your children?! Horrific. I certainly believe in disciplining your children, but when Mike and I had cause to bring correction our children knew exactly what they were being disciplined for! There is no point leaving them guessing because then they would not understand which behaviour was unacceptable. And neither do we want to permanently scar them in our discipline. We may have felt it necessary to remove a toy for a bit longer in order to make a point, but we would not take everything from them forever, or destroy things! That is beyond cruel and anyone who thinks our God is like that has a very distorted picture of who he really is.

Job is one example of someone who lost everything and it was not a sign that God did not love him. In fact, it actually was a sign that God thought very highly of his servant Job.

Since Job is the go-to book for people who have experienced some great suffering I read it again when we lost Nathan. It helped a little. It is important to remember, though, that Job is Old Covenant. By that I mean that things were different before Jesus came and we cannot insert ourselves completely into Job's story. God did not allow Nathan to die because he was boasting to Satan about *me*. I do not know why Nathan died but if there is a reason, I am sure that is not it.

This question was huge for me, the question of whether God really loved me. I longed to understand why, if God truly loved me, he did not answer my prayers for Nathan.

Loving Nathan

CHAPTER 2: BACK TO THE BEGINNING

I had good parents. They would have called themselves Christians but only because that was the culture of their day. My mother even attended church regularly: every Christmas and Easter. It was the acceptable thing. We still talked about God in schools too and I used to pray every night before I went to sleep.

As I entered my teenage years I had a lot of questions about God. I struggled to find anyone who could help me find answers about who God was, what he was like, and how I should respond to him. I thought very logically and decided that if there was a God then it would be sensible, even important for me to find out about him. In my school, if you were in the top classes you had the opportunity to speak at a school assembly. I took this as my opportunity to ask the whole school if there was anyone who could help me in my search for God. I informed everyone that I was sick of hearing what they all believed about God, I wanted to hear *why* it was that they believed. My assembly did not go over too well and the only person who responded to my pleas was the headmaster who called me into his office so that he could rebuke me for five long minutes.

Since I could not find a person to help me, I decided to read the Bible and of course I started in the obvious place—the beginning. Genesis was interesting and so was Exodus, but Leviticus!

At this point I angrily rejected my search for God.

He was just too difficult to find out about. I stopped reading the Bible and stopped asking questions. A couple of months later I went on a camping holiday with my sister and some friends. One evening we were walking around the town where we had camped, feeling a little bored. A young man approached us and asked if we would like some coffee. I was the only one of the four of us who noticed that he was carrying a big Bible with him but I did not say anything because I was happy to have found something to do. There were biscuits on offer with the coffee and then we had to sit and listen to several young people who shared with the group why they believed in Jesus. It was the exact answer to what I had asked in my school assembly but I refused to listen because I had given up on God.

My sister Linda and I had always been very close. We shared a bedroom and were often sent to bed before we were quite ready to fall asleep, so we talked together. In all the years that we chatted, however, we had never talked about God and whether he was real or not. I was taken by surprise when Linda seemed to be listening carefully to what the various young people shared in this gathering. I was even more taken aback when she said that she wanted to continue the conversation with a young couple who lived close by. Our two friends were already regular church goers, one to a Catholic Church and another to an Anglican one. They too wanted to visit with this couple. My friend who attended the Catholic Church, Dabbie, was my best friend at the time. She went to church because her parents still insisted that she attend and she had previously informed me that she did not enjoy going. The Anglican friend had a very private faith and we had never talked about Christianity. The fact that my sister, who I thought I knew really well, and my other two friends who I thought were disinterested in discussing Christianity, all wanted to continue the conversation with our new friends totally caught me off guard. I had enjoyed the free coffee and biscuits but enough was enough. I refused to go to the couple's flat with my friends and instead simply stood outside waiting for them to finish. Unfortunately, the coffee insisted I go into the flat in order to make use of their bathroom. Since I was inside I decided to show off my knowledge of the Bible. After all I had just read Genesis, Exodus and the beginning of Leviticus. Until three in the morning I challenged the beliefs of this young couple in what I considered to be a very logical fashion. The problem was that there was something about John and Maureen that was very attractive. They had an atmosphere about them that I wanted. They said it was their relationship with God. That made no sense but it was enough for me to agree to continue the conversation the next evening.

Our conversation actually continued for three or four evenings, always until the early hours of the following day. Then they invited us to join them for tea that Sunday afternoon, with the understanding that we would attend church with them afterwards. The attraction of homemade sandwiches and cake was too much for us and we all agreed to go to their church.

It was awful. When we walked in it was obvious that everyone knew each other and that they all were Christians. Then they had this message about the need to become Christians and although the pastor may have had some very valid points, I was too angry to take anything in. I was convinced that they had put the whole service together for our benefit since what was the point in telling a bunch of Christians that they needed to become Christians. After the service, someone else invited us round for a cup of tea. I was asked if I had any more questions and although I had not received satisfactory answers to many of the issues I had raised, I did not see any point in going over it all again. I told him that I had no more questions. Then he said something that appealed to my sense of logic. He told me that the only way I would ever know if Christianity was real or not was to try it. In my sleeping bag in the tent that night I prayed silently, something I had not done for several years. We had received instructions about what we needed to do so I was ready to try it. The first thing we were told was that we needed to admit we were sinners. Well I would be stupid if I did not think I was selfish, which was what I understood sinning was about, so my prayer went something like this. *"God, I don't know if you are for real or not, but if you are, I admit I'm selfish. And I am asking you to come into my life and be the boss."* That was it. What did I have to lose? If God did not exist, I had wasted ten seconds. If God did exist, I had just made the best decision of my life. Then I turned over and went to sleep.

The next morning, I felt like a light had been turned on inside me! It was the most incredible feeling. God had heard my prayer! And he had said yes. I was so happy. But I said nothing to anyone.

That evening we were saying our goodbyes to our new friends, John and Maureen, and one other young man they had brought in to help them. They were asking all four of us why we had not responded to the gospel message they had shared over so many hours we had spent together. They asked the other three first, who all gave various reasons that I no longer recall. Then they turned their attention on me. They asked me why I had not come to believe that God loved me and had sent his son to die for me. Why had I not become a Christian?

"*Actually,*" I informed them, "*I have.*"

After I had admitted that I had become a Christian, both my sister and one of my friends changed their responses and confessed that they also had asked Jesus to be the boss of their lives. My last friend who was already a regular attender at her local Anglican church did not feel the need to do anything further in her walk with God.

Chapter 2: Back to the beginning

I was so excited to feel that God loved me, that he wanted to have a relationship with me. It was a bit like I had gone to a dance and the most popular boy in the school made it clear that he wanted to dance with me, just me. I was so very happy and I was convinced that all my problems were over! After all, I had had an encounter with the living God. How could I possibly have any problems after that?

It wasn't long before I experienced the feeling of being let down by God, for the first time.

The biggest issue that I was aware of in my life was that I really hated to hear the sound of other people eating. I know it sounds funny, but it was a big deal to me. In particular, my father had given up smoking and in its place he had chosen to eat more candy. His favourite was something in the UK that we referred to as American hard gums. I think they are similar to hard jujubes. My dad and I used to sit and watch wrestling together, something he enjoyed—and I simply enjoyed spending time with him. But as he popped hard gum after hard gum into his mouth I found myself becoming more and more agitated. Now, I had been convinced that God was going to take that annoyance away from me so that I could enjoy spending time watching wrestling with my father once again. It didn't happen, and eventually I stopped watching wrestling with my dad.

Still, the excitement of entering into a relationship with the Lord Jesus was more than sufficient to overcome my annoyance at my other problems not have been dealt with. I had come to know God, to be known by him. I was loved by God. The God who created the universe and breathed life into mankind, had come to live in me—how could I not be excited?

My conversion experience was very black and white—one day I was not following God, and then one day I was following wholeheartedly after him! I was so happy. In fact, the day after I made the decision to put God first in my life I went out and had a few drinks to celebrate. I knew more joy now than I had ever experienced previously. I would not say that I had struggled with depression before I became a Christian but I was lonely and had half-heartedly attempted suicide a couple of times. They were more a cry for help than a genuine desire to end my life. I was painfully shy both at school and with extended family, and instead of being gentle and sympathetic, my mother became angry and threatened to put bars in my bedroom window to stop me from jumping out. Not that my bedroom was even high enough to do much damage to myself if I had jumped.

I wish I could say that becoming a Christian put a stop to my suicidal thoughts but it did not, and my one true attempt happened less than a year later. About six months after my initial conversion I was ready to give up. It was not that I no longer believed in God, it was because I was reading the Bible and what was happening in my life and in my church was very different to what I was reading. I was invited to a youth retreat for our small church the same weekend that I had decided to quit being a Christian and because I knew the lady who ran it was a great cook I decided to go along. I figured I could wait until after the weekend to stop being a Christian. There was just five of us young people, and this wonderful couple prayed for us to receive the Holy Spirit. We prayed, and we waited, and we prayed, and we waited, and we prayed, and so it went on for about five hours. And then the Holy Spirit came. I felt like I was drunk again only this time I had not touched a drop of alcohol. We laughed, we cried, we sang, and we enjoyed being filled with the Holy Spirit. It was so wonderful that I no longer wanted to quit being a Christian.

None of us young people spoke in tongues then which was a disappointment to me. I prayed and even fasted for three days but nothing happened. It bothered me that everything seemed so difficult in the Christian life, but there

Chapter 2: Back to the beginning

were big changes heading my way.

Every school day for seven years I had caught the bus in order to travel to my high school, the Gilberd, in Colchester, England. I carried all my books and anything else I needed, and I participated fully in my school life. That was now drawing to a close. I had chosen a university the furthest away from home. This was not because I was unhappy at home but because I wanted to make a clean break, and not travel home every other weekend. So I chose Aberystwyth, in Wales. Prince Charles went there, before me of course, and I decided that if it was good enough for him then it was good enough for me.

A month or two later I left for my first year at university. There I had the opportunity to share my experience with the Holy Spirit with some new friends, and was asked to pray for them to receive the Holy Spirit too. Of course I did so gladly. And then the unthinkable happened! Not only did my friends receive the Holy Spirit, but they were speaking in tongues too! I should have been happy for them, but instead I was wildly jealous, and angry at God.

When they left for an evening church service, I decided to pray one more time for the gift of tongues. Nothing happened so I made the decision to kill myself for real. This was not for attention this time. I was fully prepared to end my life over this issue because of what I considered it to mean: God did not love me as much as he loved my friends. The easiest and most painless way to commit suicide, in my estimation, was to swallow a lot of pills, and just go to sleep forever. I went to where I kept my aspirins and discovered I only had three of them. That would barely rid me of a headache let alone end my life, so I figured I would try one last thing before I went to find a friend and ask to borrow more aspirins. I opened my Bible and randomly placed my finger on a verse. I did not think I was supposed to do that kind of thing, but since I was about to die anyway what difference did it make. And my finger landed on a verse in Romans that said *"...use the gift you have been given."* Speaking in tongues was a gift, right? After a few minutes of speaking out whatever strange sounds came into my mind, my heart was bursting with excitement. Clearly I started praying in tongues, it wasn't just made up. My heart informed my mind that this was God!

Suicide is not something I any longer have to deal with. Perhaps even more importantly, I no longer compare myself with those around me. I have experienced God's love in my life, and I want others to experience it too. Whenever I am given the opportunity to share a message in a new situation, my first thought is always the love of God for all people, and particularly for those who have already made the choice to walk with him. I am loved by God. That is such a powerful statement. As a Christian I have not always believed that statement. The truth is, however, that I have always been loved by God, both before and after I responded to him.

CHAPTER 3: NATHAN'S BEGINNING

It has always been easier to focus on what I did not have, rather than on what I did have. I'm sure that I am not unique in this. God blessed me with a son. My journey with my son was not always filled with joy, although there were many happy moments over the years. And I was not always the positive influence on his life that I wanted to be, but he was always a blessing from God. As I have remembered more of his journey, I have been able to recognise God's love for both Nathan and myself, as we laughed together, learned together, and sometimes argued together. Whatever happened, however, God was always there for both of us. This chapter is about where it all began with Nathan.

Mike and I took the necessary steps to avoid having children during the first year of our marriage, so that we could get used to living as a couple before we had to share each other with a little person. I was finishing up a Master's degree in Pure Math. Since Mike could not find any work in his field of electronics, he took a job as an auxiliary nurse. Although I was encouraged to do further study and gain a PhD, together we prayed and felt that God was calling us into missions. We applied to work with Youth with a Mission (YWAM). Both Mike and I had experienced so much of God and we wanted to help others discover the God who loved them too.

Our initial time with YWAM was actually quite

difficult for us. We learnt a lot and our relationships with the Lord grew stronger, but unfortunately our relationship with each other nearly came to an end. During an outreach in Europe in which we had to live in a tiny tent, to be exact. We had some excellent counsellors, however, and made the right choice to stay together. From there we joined a small outreach team back in the UK. After about a year in that situation we had a falling out with our leadership and felt that we had no choice but to move on. Although we had left YWAM without any finances or supplies, and were only able to eat the first week because of the kindness of some friends, the Lord quickly opened some wonderful doors for us. We initially moved into a house that was condemned. It had a huge crack in one of the walls and we could see and feel the outside from indoors. But it was free, which was great because we had no money. Mike took a dishwashing job just to get us on our feet. From there he found a job more suited to his electronics training and I also found work. My mother helped with the down payment on a house and we soon felt established. We had found a good local fellowship and we felt ready to start a family.

Unfortunately, it was not that easy. We had fun trying but after a while we began to suspect that there was something wrong. I visited our doctor, as did Mike, and we participated in a number of tests. The results indicated that I was not ovulating. My doctor explained that he did not know what was preventing me from ovulating, and hence could not say if it was a temporary or a permanent situation. He referred me to a specialist. About a week later I received my appointment schedule, in approximately three years' time! For those who live in the UK this might not come as a surprise. The National Health System was wonderful in that it was freely available

Chapter 3: Nathan's beginning

to everyone. What was not so wonderful was the very long waits for conditions that were not life threatening.

I was disappointed but not devastated. I had been praying to get pregnant but I was enjoying all that Mike and I were able to do together and knew that some of that would stop once we had a child. I was content for life to continue as it already was. I made the decision that since we were not about to have our own children perhaps this would be a good opportunity for me to train to teach other people's children. I applied to various universities and discovered one that had the wonderful idea of three days a week in a school placement and only two days in lectures. Every university accepted my application but my first choice was the one that offered plenty of in-class experience.

Not many months into my course I discovered that I was pregnant. We had stopped trying intentionally to conceive but of course we continued to enjoy love making. Some have suggested that without the pressure to reproduce, my system relaxed and did what it was supposed to do. Maybe it was that. Maybe it was God. Whatever it was, I was now pregnant.

In the beginning of my pregnancy I felt reasonably well. I had a cup of tea and a digestive biscuit whenever I felt queasy, and that seemed to help a bit. The tiredness was a struggle but I managed to continue with my teacher training course. And as many women experience, everything began to feel a little easier after fifteen weeks. We chose some paint for the nursery and began to decorate.

I remember the day that I began to bleed. I was sixteen weeks pregnant. The whole morning I was painting the nursery. Then in the afternoon I had my antenatal appointment. Unfortunately, a lot of ladies were also at the clinic waiting to see the midwives and there were not enough chairs to go around. Those of us who were still in the early stages of our pregnancy left what chairs there were for the ladies who were nearing the date of their delivery. I was tired after painting all morning and standing for two hours while I waited to be seen was not much fun, but it could not be avoided.

Later that evening the bleeding started. Not spotting, not a few heavy drops, more like someone had turned a tap on inside me. It just seemed to pour out. I saturated three sanitary towels in less than a minute, and it kept coming. I was shaking in terror, extremely concerned as to what this all might mean, and I was so glad that Mike was home. He called the doctor, who said that I had to lie down with my feet up and that he would be around to visit as soon as possible. He was indeed very quick to come to the house but he could not be very reassuring. The baby was still very small and he had no way of knowing if he or she was still alive. I was instructed to lay on the bed with my feet higher than my head, and do nothing, not even fold the laundry. And the doctor put no time limit on how long I had to continue to do this.

"God, where are you? Why is it all going wrong? Why aren't you helping me more? Please save my baby."
The first couple of days I was very glad of the rest, if not of the reason for it. I had lost a lot of blood and I was feeling very weak and tired. After that I began counting patterns in the wallpaper and marks on the ceiling, and I hated it. I tried to pray a lot too but I was finding it very difficult to focus. I ended up oscillating between complaining to God and asking him to intervene and save my baby. The worst part was not knowing whether I still had a growing baby at all. Lying in bed all day for the sake of my baby was one thing, but lying there when perhaps

Chapter 3: Nathan's beginning

it was already too late—well that was painful. Cruel even.

On top of everything else, Mike did not know how to cook. He really didn't. It was cereal for breakfast, fish fingers and peas for lunch, and boiled eggs for supper. Then the same again the next day. And the next day. Occasionally a kind lady from our church would take pity on us and bring us a meal. Those were better days.

Eventually the doctor allowed me out of bed in order to travel and get an ultrasound, and he informed us that thankfully, the baby was fine. I had experienced placenta praevia. What that meant was that the placenta was partially over my cervix, and after my strenuous day it had come away from the wall of my uterus. Lying down with my feet raised had given the placenta the opportunity to reattach itself, and it had done so further up the uterus wall and was no longer partially over the cervix.

"Thank you, Father."

I was relieved. I was so happy to still be pregnant, but I did feel a little guilty for not trusting God more. I had experienced so much of God's love for me over the years, and yet when things went wrong in my life I struggled to trust him.

Although the doctor and the midwives were convinced that there was no longer a problem, I was now very nervous. I knew that I had nearly lost my baby in part because I had pushed myself physically, and now I was reticent to do too much. I felt too anxious to return to my teaching practice and I was ready to sacrifice my teaching certificate for the safety of my baby. Fortunately, however, because I had chosen the course with three days in the classroom all the way through, they decided I had sufficient experience to receive the certificate even though I missed several weeks at the end.

I have never been very good at sitting around. As

my baby grew inside me I became more and more confident that everything was going to be fine, so I started venturing out more. I am quite tall and being pregnant did not cause me to waddle side-to-side like a duck, as many women complain about. Many folks thought I was only about seven months pregnant when in fact I was two weeks overdue. Two weeks was also the limit set by the midwives, and I had an appointment after that to be induced. We lived just two miles from the hospital and it was a nice day, so I decided to walk there rather than have Mike drive me. When we arrived at the hospital and explained why we were there they immediately placed me in a wheelchair to be taken to the ward. It seemed quite amusing after having walked for two miles. I felt like waving at people as I was being wheeled around since I felt so happy!

Then began the process of trying to persuade this baby to leave the safety of the womb and enter the world. And he took quite some persuading! They increased whatever drug it was that they were giving me, and suddenly strong contractions set in and everything began moving very fast. It quickly became apparent that I needed an episiotomy in order to make sufficient room for the baby to exit my body, and a junior midwife was given the task. Unfortunately she was unable to cut me with the instrument handed to her, something of which I am glad I was unaware of. Another midwife promptly grabbed the scissors and the deed was done. Moments later Nathan was born!

Pethidine was the drug that they administered to me for pain relief. Since they were unaware that my baby was just about to be born I had been given quite a large dose moments before I was ready to push, and only about twenty minutes before Nathan was actually born.

Chapter 3: Nathan's beginning

Consequently, I felt out of it for quite a while afterwards. I remember lying in my bed in the ward and Mike walking in, and I was trying to work out in my mind if he had actually walked in or if I had dreamt it. I often wondered afterwards if that large dose affected Nathan too, but I guess we will never know.

In those days, new mothers were expected to stay in hospital for seven days. The nurses would teach them how to feed their babies, how to bathe them, change their nappies, and everything else that was so new and exciting. It was extremely helpful, even if in my case there were seven of us in a six-bed ward.

We had plenty of visitors, plenty of flowers, and plenty of joy at the birth of my wonderful new son. God had blessed me with a son, and I was both happy and grateful.

Loving Nathan

CHAPTER 4: HOW DOES GOD LOVE ME?

I've watched this movie a few times called Bruce Almighty. Somehow this ordinary guy gets to become God for a short period of time. Rather than listen to all the prayers, Bruce decides it would be easier to simply answer 'yes' to all of them. A little later we see people winning the lottery, many people, all winning the lottery. They won just one dollar each!

Winning the lottery is something that I have no interest in, but I would like to have a quick positive answer to my prayers. Have you ever wondered what would happen if everyone got an answer, every time? *"God, please help me to do well on this test. I know I have not studied very hard, but I am trusting you to give me the right answers."* As a teacher, I would not be very happy if God started answering those kinds of prayers for all my students. Why would any of them need to pay attention to what I was trying to teach them if they could simply hear from God to get the answers?

There may be times when we do need to pray for specific answers but it would not be appropriate to rely on God to bail us out and never bother to actually study. When I was preparing for my final exam for my Pure Mathematics degree in the UK, I sensed the Holy Spirit nudging me to study one particular section. I thought God would not do that kind of thing, so I ignored the nudging. You already know what I am going to tell you! Yes, it came up in the final exam. I received a really good mark for my bachelor's degree, but not the highest possible. I often wondered if I had responded properly to the Holy Spirit's nudging then I would have received the very best mark.

If God always answered our prayers the way we wanted him to, what would that lead to?

"Please help me to lose weight—even though I know I have eaten too much today and not done any exercise."
"Please help me to get the job that I want."
"Please help me to be more popular at school."
"Please make sure it doesn't get too hot (or cold) tomorrow."

The list is endless. And of course, there would be the prayers that are for opposite things, like a farmer praying for rain for his crops while a family is praying for sunshine so they can enjoy a picnic. Maybe God could make it rain just on the crops? It would be even more problematic when opposing football teams both ask God for a win. Unless God has a favourite football team, of course.

The bigger problem, however, would be that we only wanted God for what he could do for us. If I had a God who gave me everything I asked for I would be very fond of him! Apart from the obvious requests for health, great jobs and wonderful friends, I would probably ask for improved sports skills, and faster running ability. God would become a bit like a genie in a bottle, who would give you anything you ask for, except with more than just three wishes. In all likelihood I would begin to love God for what I could get out of him, just like Satan suggested about Job.

God is not a genie, and yet the message of

Scripture is very clear—God *does* want to bless us. The Father wants to give good gifts to his children. His desire is to bring us all to a place of completeness. He wants us to be well in soul and body. The fact that so many of us in the Body of Christ are limping along, rather than dancing in victory, is a sign that we are not walking in all that God has for us. When I was a young Christian, the message given to those who were sick and not receiving healing from the Lord seemed to be that they did not have enough faith. I believe that to be a cruel and incorrect idea. Often in Scripture it was the faith of the person praying for the sick folks that opened up the way for God to heal, rather than the faith of the person who was sick themselves. If someone in our church is not receiving a needed healing it is as much an indictment against the church community's lack of faith as it is against theirs. We need to stand with one another, pray and support one another, and especially be a source of love and encouragement towards those who are struggling physically.

At the same time, it is vitally important that we do not let our circumstances dictate to us what to believe. I have been guilty of that on many occasions. When I thought that I was going to miscarry my baby I was pleading with God for mercy. I was not praying from a place of faith, I was praying from a place of emotional hope, and I do not mean Biblical hope. Biblical hope is a confident expectation that God is going to come through for you. I was not confident, I just really wanted him to protect my baby, and allow me to carry him to term.

I did bring Nathan to term but not because of my strong faith, it was because of God's mercy. I was very grateful, and I felt that God loved me because he gave me what I had prayed for. The truth is, if I *had* miscarried

Nathan, that would not have been a sign that God didn't love me.

God had trusted me with a son. I was so very thankful! I felt loved by God. This was not just because I had been able to bring my child to term though that certainly helped. I passed God's love on to Nathan. I loved being a mother and Nathan was a wonderful baby. I even enjoyed when he woke me up for a feed in the middle of the night. I would sit there in the nursery rocking back and forth as I fed him, giving thanks to God for this delightful gift. It was a wonderful time for me, a time of peace, a time of deep joy. I was determined to be the best mother I could be and constantly place God at the centre.

How easy it is to feel loved when everything is going so well. Does God love us more at those times? We all know how ridiculous that question is, and yet so often the way we behave suggests that we do indeed think that way. God never promised us lives free from troubles. The truth is that we live in a fallen world and troubles do tend to come our way. And when they do, God still loves us. Those are the times that we need to go deeper with God and learn to recognise that circumstances should not dictate what we believe. And when we are free from troubles, we should just enjoy life. As a baby, Nathan was so much fun to be with. He was carefree and happy, and so was I.

CHAPTER 5: YOUNG FAMILY YEARS

We did not purposefully try to have another baby straight away, but neither did we take any steps to prevent it from happening. We enjoyed a good love life and nineteen months later Abigail was born. Things were a little harder now, caring for two small children. God provided for me wonderfully, however, in that Mike was unemployed for the first six months of Abigail's life. Friends and family were very concerned at our situation because finances were rather tight, but for me it was simply a wonderful blessing. While we had been missionaries we had learned to live frugally. Having the support of my husband at home was much preferable to having money for extras. We had enough to pay our mortgage, heating and buy food, and even if the food was not always very exciting it wasn't a problem for us.

As my young children began to grow it quickly became apparent that Nathan had some issues. I would ask him to pass me something... and there would be a significant delay before he responded. In fact Abigail would always respond quicker than he did, despite being nineteen months younger. It was not because he was unwilling to help, because the same delayed response would occur when I asked if he would like a biscuit or some other treat that he enjoyed. Abigail would consistently respond faster and come for the treat before Nathan seemed to understand what he was being asked. I mentioned it to the doctor whose only suggestion was a hearing test. We tried that and found Nathan's hearing to be fine.

This slowness in understanding instructions continued to become an issue when I enrolled Nathan in an activity class at the local recreation centre. The children would be told to run from one end of the gym to the other, and everyone was nearly there before Nathan even started. In a toddler that kind of thing is cute enough that everyone simply laughed and assured me that he would grow out of it.

In other areas Nathan seemed to be advanced. He loved books, and could recognise many words from as young as three years old. He had learned to read before he started school and we were able to have some great discussions together. He tended to be very gentle and caring, although I do recall one day when he had watched a cartoon on the TV and then he turned and hit his sister. He started laughing and clearly expected me to laugh with him. I realised that it had been funny on the cartoon he had just watched when someone was hurt and Nathan thought it should be funny too if he hurt his sister. That led to a little talk about the differences between cartoons and real life, and Nathan never hit his sister again.

Since we wanted our young children to experience the joy of having pets, we bought a couple of gerbils and a nice cage to keep them in. The gerbils were reasonably friendly and I permitted Nathan to touch them when I was there to supervise. I am not quite sure how it actually happened but one day I was not paying much attention and one of the gerbils fastened his teeth into Nathan's thumb. Where most young children would have screamed and shaken the gerbil loose, Nathan simply held up his thumb for me to see, the gerbil still attached, and with blood dripping from the bite. The gerbil was not releasing Nathan and he simply said, *"It's biting me Mummy."* Nathan was perfectly calm and matter of fact about the whole incident, even as it occurred. The gerbil eventually dropped from Nathan's thumb, and I made sure the wound was properly cleaned and dressed. After everything was back to normal and I looked back at what had just happened, I could not decide whether to laugh or to cry. Nathan seemed to be very different to all my friends' children. Was there something wrong with him, or was this just his personality?

Despite my concerns, I really enjoyed being a mother to both Nathan and Abigail. We had some wonderful friends in our local church, several with children of similar ages to our two. We decided to share a meal with another couple each week, with one of us providing the main course while the other would provide the desert. Their two children were slightly older than Nathan and Abigail, but the four of them had a lot of fun together. In the summer we would inflate a paddling pool in the back garden and the children and mothers would take turns running through the water, splashing anyone who came close enough. We had so much fun in those early years, and I appreciated the fact that Mike and I chose for me not to return to work, but to be able to stay home with our children. In many ways these were the happiest years of my life.

And of course, we wanted to introduce our children to the Lord Jesus as soon as they were able to have some understanding of what it meant to choose to follow him. We shared with Nathan about how Jesus died on the cross in order for him to be forgiven for every naughty thing that he had done, and how he rose again to bring Nathan life. We asked if he would like to ask Jesus to be the boss of his life and he quickly agreed. He prayed a simple prayer giving his life to the Lord and then continued with a request that Jesus be the Lord of Abigail's life too, since she was not yet able to ask him herself.

We filled those early years with a lot of activity. I preferred to be outside, and frequently took my children to the park, or down to the pond to feed the ducks. Walking anywhere seemed to take a lot of time, however. Nathan would not be hurried. It was as if he had to stop and study every blade of grass along the way. I deliberately left very early if we were walking somewhere particular, in order to avoid trying to force Nathan to travel faster than he seemed able to go.

Despite how much I was enjoying being a stay-at-home mother, Mike and I were also very much in prayer for what God wanted to do with our lives. We felt called to missions and since YWAM was our initial experience that was the organisation that we wanted to work with again. Mike had electronics training and felt that the Lord wanted to use him in that area, so he was looking into the video ministry within YWAM. When we travelled initially with YWAM through Europe we had stopped off at the base in Lausanne, Switzerland, which was where the YWAM video ministry was located at the time. He had spoken with Larry, the person in charge, and really liked both the leader and the ministry. Mike wanted to eventually go back to Lausanne and work with Larry.

We had shared with our pastor our desire to serve the Lord with YWAM, but he suggested that the time was not yet right for us to go. We recognised the wisdom of submitting to our pastor's guidance, and put the move on hold for a while. A year or so later we were in a worship meeting and Mike heard a voice behind him telling him to

Chapter 5: Young family years

go to Lausanne. He turned around to see who had spoken and there was no one there! With no one else at the meeting knowing of our interest in Lausanne, and the fact that there was no one anywhere near Mike when he heard this voice, we agreed that it must have been the Lord! Mike and I both felt stirred by the Holy Spirit to look at applying to YWAM again. Mike wrote to Larry and shared our desire to serve the Lord with YWAM. This was actually the second time that Mike had written to Larry about working with him in Switzerland, but the first one had met with a polite dismissal, since they had no need of Mike's skills at that time. After Mike wrote this letter we went to share again with our pastor. After we prayed together, our pastor agreed that the timing was now right. The very next day we received an invitation from YWAM in Switzerland, inviting us to go and work with them there. This greatly encouraged us, since our letter to them could not have even reached them before they sent us theirs. Yes, the timing was right for us to sell up and move!

A few months later we had sold our house and packed up what we had left, ready to leave for Switzerland. The children were still too young to fully understand what was going on, but I think they caught something of our excitement and accepted it as a good thing. And it *was* a good thing, both for them and for us.

I sometimes wonder what would have happened in Nathan's life if we had not left England. Was there something wrong with him, that we might have discovered if we had stayed in our own country? And if we had discovered what was wrong, would we have known how best to help him? Alternatively, if we had stayed, would Nathan have had to face a lot of bullying in the local schools? Unfortunately, young children who are not well supervised do tend to pick on someone who is different. We will never know for certain, but I think ultimately that moving to Switzerland *was* the best thing for all of us. I believe that God's love, demonstrated through other people who wanted to put God first in their lives was far more helpful to Nathan than anything we might have gained by staying in England.

Nathan did not have to attend school in Switzerland and instead went to a preschool at the YWAM base. Most of the other children were from American families although there were also a few from various parts of Europe. The teacher was also an American and the language variations caused some difficulties for Nathan. In England, the sidewalk is referred to as the pavement, while some Americans, Nathan's teacher included, refer to the road as the pavement. When the children went for a walk together, strict instructions were given to not walk on the pavement. Trying to be obedient, Nathan walked on the road. His teacher was quite upset with him but soon came to understand what was going on.

Nathan continued to excel with his reading but his handwriting was not so good. He was clearly very intelligent, but he struggled to focus on his work. He was still very young, however, so his problems tended to look more cute than worrisome. He had a couple of good years in Switzerland. He particularly loved the interactions that he had with the many young men and women who came through the base to learn how to better serve the Lord Jesus. On his birthday one year we happened to be in Spain on outreach, and one of the students put Nathan on his shoulders and carried him around encouraging everyone to wish him a happy birthday. Nathan recalled the event years later as the highlight of his birthday that year, maybe even the highlight of his year.

Chapter 5: Young family years

As our children spent hours away from home I began to desire involvement in some form of ministry myself. Switzerland had been wonderful but soon Mike and I felt that we needed more training in order to become small group leaders. There was no opportunity to do this in Switzerland, so we applied to a YWAM school in the UK and were quickly accepted. It was hard packing everything up again; even though we lived in just two rooms, we seemed to have accumulated more stuff. We thinned things out again and said goodbye to all of our friends. The children did not complain and we did our best to keep those items that were important to them. We travelled by train to Paris and from there we crossed the city to another train station for a connection that would take us to the coast, where we would catch a ship across the channel to the UK. We must have looked quite comical in France, trying to get four suitcases, a buggy (stroller), several small bags, and the four of us into a small Renault. I could not quite work out if the driver of the Renault was feeling sorry for us or was frustrated with us, as we squeezed another plastic bag down the side of our suitcases in the back seat. Mike had the front seat, and I shared the back with two children, two suitcases, and the buggy. I was glad that it was a relatively short journey! We managed not to lose anything on the way, which was really quite incredible, and soon we were back in England.

Nathan was now of an age where he was required to attend school. It was not a good experience for him. It was a small village school, and the principal and teachers were all very welcoming, but Nathan was not a typical boy of his age. His teacher complained to us that she would give instructions to the class which Nathan never seemed to understand. He had to be told again, individually, before he would do anything. I am not quite sure what she expected us to do about it, since we were dealing with similar issues at home. The only suggestion that they came up with was to have his hearing tested once again. We complied, but the results were the same as before—there was nothing wrong with Nathan's hearing.

Something even more difficult began to happen also, and that was bullying. It is sad the way that children seem to pick on each other, and particularly on anyone who is different. Unfortunately, Nathan was the different child and very often the other children were not kind to him. One little boy in particular kept trying to push Nathan around. Out of frustration, one-day Nathan simply pushed the boy over and then sat on him. All he was trying to do was stop the boy from hitting him. Of course, Nathan was the one who ended up in trouble.

We did have one beautiful breakthrough at this time. Nathan was not talking about what he was going through at school, even though I tried to ask a lot of questions and make sure I was available for him to talk to me. We shared with some of the other parents there, and also prayed with our small group for him. One person suggested an American game called 'The Ungame.' It was not a win or lose game, but rather one where you travelled around the board and depending on what square you landed on, you could ask, or be asked, a question. Because it was a game, Nathan happily participated and began to answer such questions as *"When was a time you felt lonely?"* or *"Tell about a time when you felt loved."* It was extremely helpful for Nathan and the rest of the family enjoyed it too. Around that time we also introduced a chart for both of our children and they would get check marks for certain behaviours and chores. For Nathan he would get a check mark for giving his parents a hug, something that he did not chose to do otherwise. These two things were such an encouragement for us and we felt that the Lord was beginning to answer our prayers for our son. We did not stay beyond our six-month YWAM school, however, and from there we joined a ministry in London.

Being back in the UK, since Nathan was now a bit older, we were becoming more aware that his difficulties were not something he was going to quickly grow out of. It is really hard for a mother to see her child struggling. There we were in a wonderful Christian community, surrounded by people who believed God could do anything, and I had a son who was being rejected at school. We were praying for students to be healed from rejection in their lives, while at the same time it was happening to my son.

"God, please help Nathan. Heal him. Set him free. Help him to make friends his own age." Nathan was featuring more and more in my prayer life.

YWAM had its own elementary school in London which was an incredible blessing for Nathan and a relief for his parents. The leaders had tried other forms of outreach into the area without any significant success, and then felt led to start a school. I am not sure how successful the school was in touching the neighbourhood but it was a tremendous blessing for the Christian families located near to it. The classes were very small, the discipline very strong, and the love for the children even stronger. Nathan continued to demonstrate unusual behaviour but the teachers ensured that he was not bullied because of it. On one occasion, the children were changing for some physical activities outside, and because Nathan was taking a long time, the other children went outside with the teacher. Nathan was instructed to join them as soon as he was changed. By the time he was actually ready, the rest of the class was returning indoors from their activities.

This would normally be something that would cause the other children to tease him, to make fun of him, but not at this school.

In this school the children were taught to be kind to one another, and the classes were small enough that the teacher could ensure they actually were. So rather than being bullied, Nathan had some friends. *"Thank you, God."* I would make the effort too, to visit other families with boys of his age and give them an opportunity to play together. Also, our team leaders had three children, two of whom were the same ages as Nathan and Abigail, so it was often convenient to have the children all together in one location. Most of the time they got on very well together, though the girls ended up much closer than the boys. No complaints from me, I was just happy that my son could actually play with other children.

Nathan performed reasonably well academically at this school, but he had great difficulties staying on task. He would often appear to be away somewhere in his own little world, and he struggled to focus on his school work. Consequently, when our team was moving a little further away and our leaders decided to start our own school, I was quite excited. The classes were going to be even smaller, with just two or three children working together. In this situation, Nathan was going to receive more one-on-one attention which would not give him the opportunity to disappear so much into his own world.

It was very encouraging to me at this time that as Mike and I were choosing to serve the Lord in missions, Nathan was receiving probably the best possible education. It was great for Abigail too, but I think she would have thrived wherever she went to school.

We lived in a slightly dangerous part of London, which had both positive and negative aspects. In most of

Chapter 5: Young family years

London, if someone tried to preach the Gospel on the streets, they would likely get moved along by the police. On at least one occasion, other YWAMers had spent a night in jail for attempting to preach in a public place. Where we were, however, the police did not interfere. There had been many race riots in this area and out of concern that something might flare up again the police tended to turn a blind eye to street meetings including, of course, street evangelism.

Our desire was to reach the people of our neighbourhood with the Gospel. We talked with people on the streets, and when possible, shared our lives with them, helping them to walk free of bad habits. Prayer was a huge part of this ministry and Nathan would pray along with us for different people we met. One time we were travelling across town in our car and Nathan began to weep. He had seen an old man pushing a cart, and the man was obviously not healthy. Nathan was very concerned that this man should have the opportunity to know the love of Jesus before he died, and his heart was breaking for him. We prayed together for the man, but unfortunately there was no way that we could stop and try to talk to him. Nathan had a very tender heart and he obviously cared deeply for those who were hurting.

We always encouraged our children to question their faith and not simply accept everything that their parents taught them. Nathan was very philosophical and he thought deeply about many subjects. Once I had a conversation with him about whether it was right for a Christian to be a spy since spies have to lie. We went back and forth on that one for perhaps an hour and a half.

During those young years I was relieved that Nathan fully embraced what we were trying to do. He believed what we believed. We prayed together as a family, we read the Bible together, we sang worship songs together. Sometimes it was a little frustrating as we had to wait on Nathan to choose a song, or to pray out loud, or simply to refocus on what we were doing, but generally those were good times for us all. Mike and I worked with people who embraced us as a family. Nathan was not a typical little boy but our friends accepted his differences. He did attend Cub Scouts for a while but did not do well in that environment. Boys of his own age, without teacher or parental guidance, were intolerant of his slowness. Nathan really had the best possible environment in a Christian school with classes of two or three students. Then in his free time he was surrounded by his family and young people who loved the Lord, and who therefore made the choice to love him too.

I longed for Nathan to overcome his difficulties and I prayed to that end. Through it all though, God provided the best possible environment for him. Had we not joined YWAM Nathan would have attended a public elementary school and despite the best efforts of his teachers he would likely have been bullied terribly. God proved himself faithful to both Nathan and his parents at this time. And yet, as I regularly explained to the Lord, it would have been so much better if he was just healed.

CHAPTER 6: LIFE IN AMSTERDAM

What does it mean to feel loved by God? For Mike and I at that time, we wanted to live our lives doing what God wanted us to. That would not have been the case if we thought God did not care about us personally. We felt loved because God was providing for us as a family, financially as well as with some great friendships and ministry opportunities. We saw some exciting results of our ministry as well; people understanding God better, and wanting to please him more. The more we experienced, the more we wanted to continue to serve God in whatever way he wanted us to.

    There was never any pressure on us to continue working with YWAM, in fact the opposite was closer to the truth. When I had first met Mike, my mother was not very happy with the relationship. We had gotten engaged very quickly and in retrospect I am not surprised my parents were concerned. Mike was serving in the army at the time and since I chose to spend Christmas with him in Germany where he was stationed, she was a little angry. She wrote me a letter referring to me as a 'camp follower,' a term for women who followed an army in order to serve as prostitutes. Not long after my father died, however, she quickly made amends and welcomed Mike into the family. She had been confident to speak out her displeasure when she had a husband to stand with her but now she did not want to be left all alone. For the same reason, she was not happy that Mike was not working to support his family. In YWAM every person has to raise their own financial support and thankfully we always had enough, but we could have had a lot more if Mike had actually been earning a living. My mother asked questions and often suggested a different occupation for Mike and myself, but she was never openly rude again.

Neither of our families could understand why we would want to help those less fortunate than ourselves, especially in other countries. They would have preferred we stay close to home, build ourselves a nice place to live, and make sure that our children had a stable financial future. Mike's mother was on her own too, since his father died when he was just thirteen. She made strong suggestions herself but never took a strong stand against what we wanted to do. For Mike and I, our desire to please God came above everyone else. We wanted our children to experience God's love too, and also to recognise that serving him might mean moving around the world.

Our YWAM leaders in London were a delightful couple from New Zealand, and while we were there with them they had three wonderful children. They were not exactly conventional leaders or parents, and did not like to always follow the rules. I was told once that to park a car where there was a yellow line (indicating no parking) was not breaking the law, it was simply saying that you were willing to pay the fine if you got caught. I enjoyed their quirky leadership more than Mike did. He loved order and knowing what was coming next. That was not available on this team. Not surprisingly Mike began to look for a different location in which to continue to serve the Lord.

We had lived in London for over three years and between us we had many friends. When the door opened

Chapter 6: Life in Amsterdam

for Mike to return to the YWAM video ministry, which was now located in Amsterdam, Abigail was devastated. She cried desperately, declaring that she would never see her best friend again. Nathan, on the other hand, did not seem to be bothered. Sometimes it seemed that he enjoyed adult company more than that of children his own age. He did have friends, but he did not express any strong disappointment to be moving away from them.

Nathan was ten at the time of this move and was now ready to attend a larger school. To this day, the Dutch allow any group to start their own education facility, and consequently there was a reasonably sized Christian elementary school available. There were many other YWAM children already attending this school, most of whom again were American, and Nathan and Abigail quickly made friends. The school was, of course, all in the Dutch language, but children learn new languages much faster than adults. We quickly realised that Nathan was particularly gifted in language learning, and where most of the English-speaking children learned sufficient Dutch to adequately communicate, Nathan insisted on always getting everything exactly correct. In fact, by the time we had been there a year, Nathan was able to act as a translator at the occasional youth gathering.

One of the first sights in Amsterdam that surprised me was of an older man, who was perhaps sixty years, cycling with his wife of similar age perched on a bar at the front of his bicycle. Seeing how confidently they both sat on the bike it was obvious that they had been doing this for years. Everyone seemed to travel by bicycle, I guess partly because the Netherlands is so flat. All the children rode their bikes to school, except for the smaller ones who ride on child seats on their parent's bike. So we purchased bikes for Nathan and Abigail. We assumed that they would be the same as those we were used to in England, so I told Nathan to jump on his bike and ride it around. Riding it was not a problem, but when he looked for the brakes he could not find them and he rode right into a metal gate. In England, bicycles typically had brakes on the handlebars and when you wanted to stop you just squeezed them with your hand. Apparently in the Netherlands in order to stop your bike you have to peddle backwards. Fortunately, Nathan was not hurt and he and Abigail cycled to school every day.

The most natural friendships for Nathan were among the sons of the other members of the YWAM video ministry, three American boys and one Dutch young man. Since the parents were often doing things together it worked well for the children to hang out. Not all of them wanted to do the same things though, and they never became very close. Nathan asked one of the boys to share secrets together and was told that he could tell his secrets if he wanted, but there was no way was this boy going to share anything private with Nathan.

Nathan continued to have problems focusing on his work at school, although he did manage to get some things done. Abigail, on the other hand, was a wonderful student and all her teachers loved her. Nathan's teacher even asked Mike and I if she was really his sister. At his urging we arranged for Nathan to see a psychiatrist since there were a couple of psychiatrists from the United States who were a part of YWAM, and they were willing to try and help. Nathan met with the doctor a couple of times and then we all met together. At this meeting we were told basically what we already knew, that Nathan was very intelligent but he had problems focusing on the world around him. She suggested that Nathan put an elastic band around his wrist and then ping himself whenever he found his mind wandering away from his school work. This seemed to be a reasonable suggestion but it's effectiveness depended completely on Nathan. He refused to do it because he did not want to inflict pain on himself. Things continued at school in the same way as before, Nathan doing just a fraction of what he was supposed to do while the rest of the time he appeared to be deep in thought about other things.

Around that time I gave birth to our third child, Hannah Ruth. Midwives are very respected in the Netherlands and it was common place to have a baby at home. We prepared everything for the delivery at home, but when I went into labour the midwife encouraged me to go to the local hospital instead. There was not a problem, it just looked like the baby was not coming in a hurry, and I think the midwife did not want to have to stay up all night. Abigail was spending the night at some friends, so we just needed to find a babysitter for Nathan. He was happy that we were going to the hospital because he found hearing my groans rather disturbing. The midwife drove me to the hospital and transferred my care to a doctor. Hannah was born at about six in the morning and four hours later I was on my way home with a new daughter.

Both Nathan and Abigail loved having a baby sister, and they would take turns holding her. I enjoyed having a third child too, although it meant for a while she was my main focus. I did try and make sure that I spent some time with my other two children, and one of the things I wanted to do with Nathan was to encourage him to play some sports. All of the boys his age loved to play baseball, so I decided I would try and introduce Nathan to the game. I had never played baseball before either, since it is not a game that we played growing up in

England, but I had a basic understanding of the rules. I would throw the ball towards Nathan and he would try and hit it. Unfortunately, one time my aim was a little off and instead of going in the direction of his bat, the ball hit Nathan on his head. He refused to play with me after that.

I tried hard to make life fun for all of my children. While Abigail enjoyed having many friends around, Nathan did not seem that interested. Even on his birthday he would rather have one friend, and quietly play Lego with him, rather than a loud exciting party with lots of gifts. Nathan continued to enjoy adult company, especially young men who would take the time to talk with him. One person in particular, Paul, was working with the YWAM video team for just a year, learning the trade as he went along. He was the son of a couple we had know many years earlier, and when he had a free evening he preferred to hang out in our apartment rather than his own. His parents were living in Canada at the time and they were leaders of the YWAM base in Cambridge, Ontario. Many years previous to this we had visited an elementary school in England where Paul's father was the vice principal. He had put together a wonderful drama about creation through to the resurrection of Jesus, called *Toymaker and Son*, and the elementary school children performed it. It was an incredible production and now adults were performing it. It had become a powerful evangelistic tool. Paul's father had gathered together many arts performers at the YWAM base there in Ontario and it began to sound like an exciting place to be.

One of the problems we encountered in Amsterdam was that there was little opportunity for me to get involved in ministry. My heart was for discipleship and some evangelism but because we lived away from the main base it was not possible for me to be involved in the training schools running there. Our hope was that in Canada both Mike and I would have opportunities to pursue what we felt God had laid on our hearts. Mike had a vision to establish a video training ministry as part of the base in Cambridge and my desire was to be involved in discipleship.

    We prayed together as a family, and agreed that the Lord was leading us to Canada. Paul had already returned there and since both Nathan and Abigail enjoyed his company so much it made moving across the Atlantic a little easier for them. Again, Abigail was very sad to be leaving her friends behind in Amsterdam while Nathan did not seem to be bothered. We packed everything up, ready for our biggest move yet.

Nathan was a cute little boy!

He loved the beach (just like his Mum!)

He had a lot of fun as a child

As he aged, he clearly loved the Lord, and music, and his sisters (especially the youngest one!)

Family, Nathan's baptism, and his love for music.

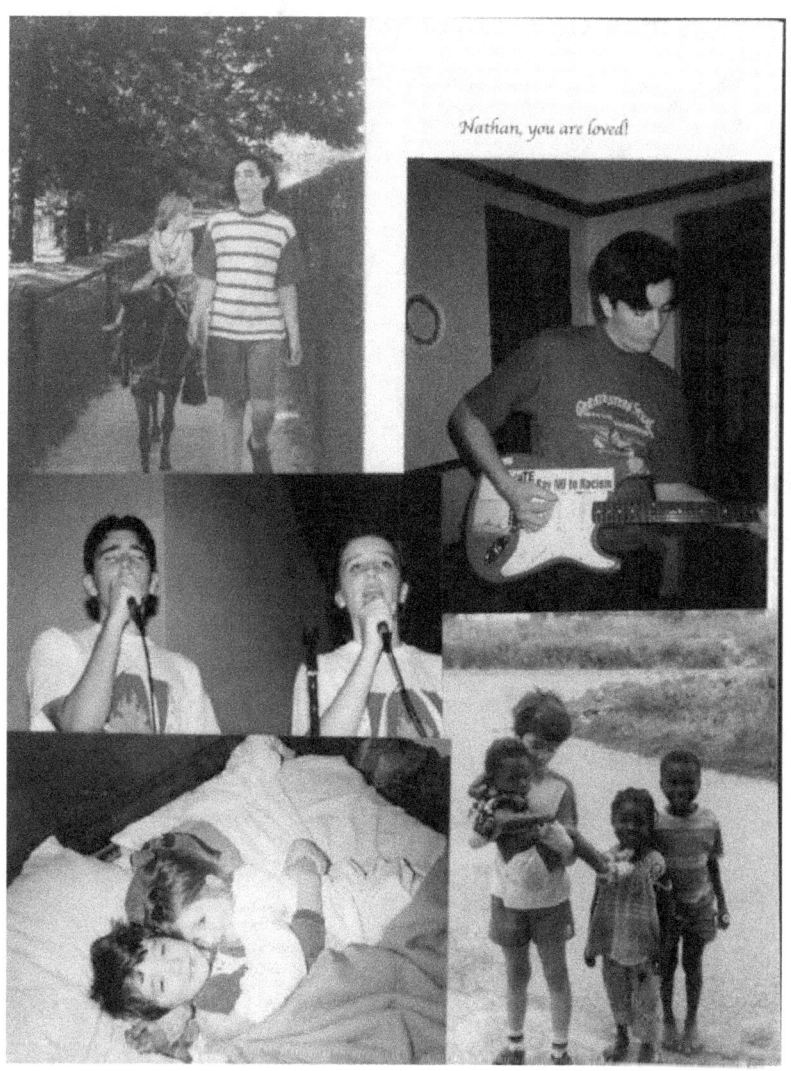

CHAPTER 7: CANADA

I had high hopes for our new start in Canada and what a great start it was. God demonstrated his love for us as a family by putting it on someone's heart to gift us with one thousand dollars when we arrived in the country. This gift came completely out of the blue and it was a wonderful blessing to help us start life in our new home.

Since we arrived in August, we had a few weeks to sort out which school Nathan and Abigail were to attend. We had been spoilt in the Netherlands where the Christian school was paid for by the government. We visited a couple of Christian schools in Cambridge and at one of them in particular we liked what we saw. Then we were informed how much it cost. Our support was not very high. In fact, even if we had put all the money we had coming in towards our kids' education, it would not have been sufficient to pay for their tuition at this Christian school. Consequently, we had to look further afield.

In the UK we were used to there being just two options, public education and Church of England education. It was not so different in Canada, although instead of Church of England the other option was Roman Catholic. To us, it seemed the options were Christian or not Christian, and therefore we chose to investigate the Catholic school system. We were very impressed with the principal of the local Catholic elementary school, especially when he offered to pray with us. It was going to cost a little to send Nathan and Abigail there but nothing like what it would cost to send them to the private Christian school that we had liked. So they were enrolled at Christ the King and began not many days later.

It was not long before we were asked to come and talk to the principal again. Nathan's first problem was that he seemed to assume that since everyone spoke English they would have the same sense of humour as in England. That was the principal's take on the situation anyway but Mike and I knew that it was more than simply a clash of cultures. Nathan had never really been able to get on well with children his own age. One of his biggest issues was that he could not read other people well, he could not understand when they were laughing at him instead of with him.

Nathan's teacher had a husband who was dying of cancer. She had very little patience for a young man who stared out of the window instead of focusing on his work, and neither did she protect him when other children picked on him. He tried being the class clown for a while, being silly instead of arguing back to the teacher. This did not work out well for him. The principal suggested that we send Nathan for a psychiatric assessment and since we had no other ideas, we agreed.

The results were not helpful, since they really just identified the problems without offering any solutions. They identified Nathan as 'socially retarded,' and they told him so. What is a thirteen-year old supposed to do with that kind of information. It was cruel.

This was a very painful time for me and I asked God why he was not helping Nathan to make the changes that he needed to make. I recognised, of course, that this was a difficult time for Nathan's teacher also, but I felt that the school should be considering the needs of my son too. Where was the help that God was supposed to offer to those who cried out to him, and where was the help of the education system? Nobody seemed to be on Nathan's side except me.

In the end I felt that I was left with no other choice than to withdraw Nathan from the school and teach him at home. He and I had a good relationship and I was a trained teacher after all, so it seemed to be the best solution. Even the principal agreed with this idea, since it was clear that the majority of Nathan's class had pretty much turned against him, and to make Nathan continue in that situation would not have been a positive experience.

In the midst of all this, however, Nathan did have some friends close to his own age. One young man from the school somehow connected with Nathan and they would get together every now and again to play with his Lego. Also, the son of our pastor recognised a need in Nathan, and tried to make a connection with him. At least it was something.

Loving Nathan

CHAPTER 8: THE TEENAGE YEARS

Rejection from your peers is always hard to live with, and Nathan received a lot of it. Having just about his whole class reject him must have been very painful for him. I think the hardest part of it all was when they told him that he was not capable of getting on with children his own age and that the rejection was really his own fault. At the same time it was clear that God brought love and acceptance into Nathan's life from other sources. We were living in a community with many young people who wanted to put God first in their lives, and some of them recognised Nathan's needs during this painful period and they worked to embrace him.

Home schooling did not turn out to be as bad as I had anticipated. Of course I knew that Nathan required a lot of help focusing on his work, and there were times when I left him for a short while in order to do some housework, only to return and find that he had done nothing. If I sat beside him though, and constantly asked him what he needed to do next, he did actually make some progress. The time alone with him also gave me the opportunity to explore different ideas to try and get him to work. I had read several articles and also some parenting books. Initially I tried the strong hand approach and threatened him with withdrawal of some privileges if he did not get a certain amount completed in a specific time. That turned out to be quite a pain, with very little positive results, and left me feeling like a villain. Then I tried the idea of praising his achievements, however small they were. I cannot say that brought any greater success but it certainly left both of us feeling better at the end of the day.

Since Nathan had been enrolled in the Catholic School Board when I had chosen to take him out of school, they deemed it necessary after a few months to send someone around to ensure that Nathan was being adequately educated at home. I showed the man all the work that I had managed to cajole Nathan into completing and he told me that it was insufficient. I found this incredibly ironic, considering it was far more than he had done while attending school the previous year. Of course, I smiled and informed this official that I would work at increasing the amount for Nathan, knowing full well that there was no way I could get more out of him without sitting beside him for most of the day.

During this period of time we were living in community at the YWAM base in Cambridge. This meant that although we had our own private quarters, at least two meals a day were shared with everyone in the dining room. We would try and keep together as a family during meal times by sitting on the same table, but there was always room for others to join us and we encouraged this. It was a great place for our three children. We had times later to discuss personal issues, but meal times were spent sharing with others what we all had been doing and learning that day.

At the base we had the ministry for performing arts, but there was also a teen and child evangelism group. The leader of the group had the attitude that it was wrong to focus on leading other young people to the Lord while neglecting the young people living among us. They had a

Chapter 8: The teenage years

strong value for discipleship and they led a vibrant youth group. This was such an encouragement for us as a family, and Nathan and Abigail loved the friendships afforded to them through this group. There were also other young people living on the base with their parents, giving our children access to positive young folks their own age. All things considered this was a wonderful environment for our two eldest children to enter into their teenage years. "Thank you, Father."

I was very grateful for all that God was providing for Nathan, and yet I longed to see more evidence that things were actually changing inside him. I prayed so much for him, and desperately tried to persuade him to make more effort himself, but I saw no real changes.

After a year of homeschooling, Nathan and I agreed that it would be good for him to try public education again. It would be his first year of high school and he chose to move out of the Catholic system. Abigail was going to continue her education later at the Catholic High School, and she was very relieved to be attending a different school from her brother. Abigail had always been a perfect student, working hard and being pleasant to teachers and students alike. It had been hard for both of them to be compared by various teachers and both were happy that this was no longer going to be the case.

One of the joys of attending a high school of some two thousand students, after an elementary school of three hundred, was the greater likelihood of Nathan finding others similar to himself. Although several other children from the community where we lived attended the same high school as Nathan, they rarely had the same classes. That was not a problem, since Nathan began to find his own friends, and he did much better socially than he had done in his previous school.

"Thank you God, this is an answer to many prayers."

Academically, however, the same problems continued to be an issue. His teachers tended to either get very frustrated with him, and consequently did not like him much, or they found him endearing and tried their best to help him be successful. He was a very pleasant young man and he always spoke politely, but he would not get his work done and often looked like he was somewhere else. Some of his classmates suggested that he was on drugs, but that was definitely not the case. At least not yet.

Nathan had been trying to play the guitar for a while, with the help of different people at the YWAM base. He was becoming quite accomplished, although he struggled when he took guitar as a course at school. The teacher complained to me that he would not listen to her in class, and preferred to play his own music rather than that which she had provided him with. Naturally that was not a surprise to me. I was so happy to see Nathan do so well at something, and I loved listening to him as he sang and worshiped the Lord in his bedroom. In fact, when the school had an evening coffeehouse, Nathan played a couple of worship songs for the audience and shared his love for the Lord. He got in a little trouble afterwards for speaking out positively about Jesus but that did not bother him. He did the same thing the next year too. Both times he was warmly received by the audience.

I was very proud of Nathan during this time, and was so encouraged by his stand for the Lord in his school. It was beautiful to see him express his love for God in worship, and I was grateful for the opportunities he was embracing.

Although Nathan loved to perform with his guitar,

Chapter 8: The teenage years

I think his greater skill was in his songwriting. He wrote one song called *"I hate Baptists."* It was, of course, tongue in cheek, because his best friend at school was a Baptist, but Nathan struggled with some of what he perceived as legalism on his friend's part, so he wrote a song about it. When his little sister complained that he never wrote a song for her, he included a new verse *"I hate vegetables."* I was not the only person who considered Nathan to be gifted in the area of music and he received many accolades both for his songwriting and his performances.

Even though Nathan was doing so much better socially at school, he continued to struggle with his work. Despite the fact I was no longer his official teacher, one semester I spent at least an hour with him every night in order to help him with his math. Then we would argue about whether he should be permitted to go out with his friends when he had not completed his homework. As Mike and I tried to insist that his school work had to come first, he would counter with the argument that he needed to have fellowship in order to stay strong in his relationship with the Lord. There was some truth in that, and sometimes we gave in, but mostly we insisted that he had to get his work done. Our hope was that he would learn to get it done quickly, but it never happened.

Not only did Nathan have access to some wonderful young Christian men and women at the YWAM base, we were also attending a local Vineyard Church and there were many other young people there too. One of the pastor's sons made a particular effort to make Nathan feel welcome, though unfortunately Nathan didn't really understand. In particular he did not seem able to read situations very well, in regards to the responses of other people. Since this young man had reached out to Nathan, he gave him a lot of attention in return, probably too much attention. I remember when I was a teenager, and I would arrive home from school only to spend the next half hour speaking to my best friend on the phone. It didn't concern me when Nathan would want to do the same with his new friend. Sadly, it was too much, too quick, and Nathan's friend tried to withdraw.

There were opportunities to get involved in King's Kids too, a Christian children's outreach program, run by YWAM. Nathan prayed with us and felt that the Lord did indeed want him to be a participant. It was obvious that the Lord touched him in these different outreaches that we attended with King's Kids over the years, but they also caused quite a bit of tension. On one such outreach there were only a few showers, and a limited supply of hot water. It was decided that each person would only be permitted three minutes in the shower. Unfortunately, Nathan was never very good at self-discipline, and when it came to his turn for a shower, he was in there for over fifteen minutes. People pounded on the shower door, saying that his time was up. He simply ignored them. The leader was very upset with him and wanted to send him home from the outreach. Since Mike and I were leaders on the same outreach, I informed her that one of us would have to leave too, which seemed to upset her even more. She insisted that we should find a neighbour to look after him, something which we were not willing to do, even if it had been a possibility. I suggested that for the rest of the outreach Nathan would be made to go last for a shower, resulting in him having only slightly warm water, at best. This seemed to be a satisfactory solution, and Nathan continued on. He was not the only uncooperative young man on that outreach, there were two other boys near his age who clearly struggled to fully obey the leaders as well. Nathan felt singled out as the worst of the three,

Chapter 8: The teenage years

which did not help. Since Nathan had strong Christian parents, I suspect more was expected of him. Sadly, Nathan tended to focus more on the rejection that he felt from the leader rather than on what he had done to deserve her disappointment.

I know that the Lord ministered both to and through Nathan on these outreaches, but a problem that remained was his seeming inability to push himself, either to do things quicker, or to improve his standards of organisation. He willingly participated in the chores, but at a much slower pace than kids even several years younger than him.

On one of our King's Kids outreaches I was given the position of spiritual director, which provided the opportunity to read the applications of all the children. This also meant I could read what previous leaders had to say about my own children. I have to admit when I read the former evaluations of Nathan they were not very encouraging. Basically, he was seen to be very self-centred and I had to admit he did seem to be overly concerned with his own needs and wants. I wondered how we had failed to instil in our son an attitude of wanting to serve others. We had worked diligently, when he was younger, to ensure that he had chores to perform. Mike particularly had demonstrated a heart of service to those around him, but somehow this had not been enough to make any difference in Nathan.

In my prayers at this time I was asking God how I might help my son to care more for the needs of others. I longed to know how best to help him, but other than asking God to do it, I didn't know what else to do.

Back at home there was growing friction between Nathan and the rest of the family. If he wanted to spend twenty minutes in the bathroom before school, brushing his long hair and grooming himself, he would do so without any concern that his sister needed to have some time to get ready also. He did not see the need to get his schoolwork done on time or keep clothes off the floor. This last one was quite a challenge for us since our apartment was too small for a family of five and Nathan's space was actually meant to be a hallway. When the YWAM base leaders had to walk through at one point, we were strongly criticised for not making Nathan keep his room tidy. By this point we had realised that we needed to pick our battles with him, and keeping his room tidy was just not on the top of our list.

Nathan continued to have some good relationships with others on the base, for which we were very grateful. We felt that this was God's provision for Nathan, who needed a lot of support. He had suffered so much rejection, and having so many people who loved and accepted him in this environment was wonderful. It sometimes took quite a lot of maturity to continue to be loving towards Nathan, however, and some of the students in the discipleship schools were not always successful in that area. When I was one of the leaders on a discipleship school outreach, we took all our children with us. Because he was a teenager, Nathan slept with some of the other guys, and his self-centred behaviour rubbed a couple of them the wrong way. At one point, when Nathan was being disrespectful of the home that had been very kindly made available for us to use, one young man had to be held back from punching him. That was the last outreach that we went on as a family.

Due to some financial difficulties, YWAM had to sell the base that we were living on, and so everyone had to move out. With our oldest two children in high school, we didn't feel we should move to another YWAM base,

Chapter 8: The teenage years

so we looked around for other accommodation. This did not prove to be easy, and after a while we were the only people left living on the base. The only humans, that is. I guess some of the doors had been left open, or maybe the windows, because somehow squirrels had found their way into the building. Nathan and I had a lot of fun walking through what was left of the base, trying on costumes that had been left behind, and making sure we did not get too close to any of the wildlife that was beginning to make their home inside rather than outside. Being the only ones left was really not much fun though, and we prayed hard for the Lord to open up somewhere else for us to live.

With the help of a contact at our church, we eventually moved into subsidised housing. There were four bedrooms and we thought it absolutely fantastic. It was surprising to us that we were offered this house because another local family had turned it down since they considered it was not big enough, and that family was the same size as ours. I guess they were not as desperate as we were.

One of the first things we did now that we were no longer living in community was to get a cat. Abigail and I went to the Cambridge Humane Society and chose a gorgeous, grey cat who seemed to immediately take a liking to Abigail. Unfortunately, when we returned home with the cat she was obviously not so enamoured with Mike and Nathan. We assumed that she had been abused by a man, and was consequently much more careful around them. Abigail named her Joplin, after the piano player Scott Joplin. We decided to trial her for a few weeks, before making it permanent, and so we put off spaying her.

Joplin spent a lot of time hiding behind the couch, so when I noticed that she was putting on weight, I assumed it was because she was not getting much exercise. Gradually she began to accept Mike and Nathan, and we decided that she was with us to stay. I took her to the vet in order to have her spayed, but as soon as I got back home after dropping her off there, the phone rang. The receptionist informed me that there was something wrong with my cat—she was pregnant. In fact she was very pregnant, close to giving birth. So I drove back to the vet to pick her up, and the next day she gave birth to five kittens on Abigail's bed. After a few weeks we managed to find homes for three of the kittens, and kept two of them. Now we had three cats.

As Mike and I searched hard for paid work, Nathan and Abigail continued to attend their high schools. Both of our older children appeared to be handling life reasonably well and did not seem adversely affected by having to move away from everyone at the base. Another King's Kids outreach came up, and we all prayed about being part of it. We continued to attend the Vineyard Church and participated in various programs that they had available, so it did not seem foolish to suggest that Nathan come with us. There was no pressure put on him to participate in Kings' Kids however, the choice was completely his own. This time he chose to stay at home, and that was actually quite convenient for us. Since we now had three cats, Nathan could look after them.

When we arrived home with Abigail and Hannah after the outreach Nathan was nowhere to be found. Then we called for the cats, but only two of them appeared, and they were significantly thinner than when we had left. We searched for the third cat, but were unable to find her. Then we tried calling some of Nathan's friends, trying to find out what was going on. No one seemed to know where Nathan was, but we did learn something of what had happened to the cats. The news was very sad. It seemed that Nathan had failed to feed them sufficiently, and one of the kittens had died. One person suggested that something was wrong with the cat who died, but it seemed likely that it had actually starved to death. Nathan had been devastated, and someone had found him sobbing uncontrollably in a corner at church the previous day. This was before any of us had cell phones, and he had been unable to receive help from anyone he had managed to reach on the landline. Sadly Nathan just didn't realise that he was not giving them enough food. This was probably as much my fault as his, since I had given clear instructions on how much to give them every day, and he was reticent to stray from what he'd been told. The main issue, however, was that it never occurred to Nathan that when he went on a sleepover, which he did twice, he needed to leave extra food for the cats. He returned after not being there for a day, and just gave them food for that day. Joplin and one of the kittens took what they needed, and the other kitten did not get sufficient to survive. He had buried her himself in the woods nearby and given her a little ceremony.

Although nobody would give us any information about where we could find Nathan, we tried to pass on the fact that we were willing to forgive him. Someone must have conveyed this message to him, because after a few hours a very distraught boy returned home. We quickly assured Nathan that we did not blame him for what happened and were simply glad that he was okay. Although we were relieved that we were all together again as a family, I struggled to understand how Nathan could neglect his responsibilities with the cats and leave them alone, twice, for more than twenty-four hours. I knew that he was very upset over what transpired, but I wondered how much he recognised that it was a consequence of his own lack of care.

While he was still at high school things were going relatively well. He had friends there, and for a while he ran the Christian Union, together with his Baptist friend. With a couple of other friends from Vineyard he walked around the school one weekend, praying for all the teachers and students there. The police stopped them, wondering what they were doing, and Nathan was not sure if they actually believed they were simply praying. Either way, they were asked to move on, so they found somewhere else to pray together.

At the same time, Nathan continued to struggle with his school work. He was doing more without a lot of coercion from us, but not sufficient to do well. I spoke with many of his teachers, asking them to be merciful with Nathan and give him another opportunity to get his work done. With a lot of help he eventually he graduated.

Mike and I attended Nathan's graduation, but he really wanted to celebrate with his own friends. He had asked some of them to meet him at a local pub, but when he arrived they were not there. This was a great disappointment for my boy, who considered his friends more important than his family. He drank a few beers anyway and sang some karaoke, which was some compensation for him.

Nathan had not enjoyed being in school. It was a relief for him to finally be finished with that period of his life. It was something of a relief of his parents too.

CHAPTER 9: FINDING EMPLOYMENT IS EASY, RIGHT?

Coming up next was his biggest challenge—finding work. I had encouraged Nathan to apply to the local college for something like personal support worker. He was very patient with people who had any form of disability, and I felt that would be a job that he could do well at. Unfortunately, when we had offered to provide Nathan with driving lessons he declined. He said that he did not trust himself to drive a car. Being a personal support worker necessitated having a vehicle and being able to drive it, so there was no point in us trying to force him in that direction.

Education had not come easily for Nathan, and he was happy to be leaving school behind. He had, however, talked about going to Oxford University in the United Kingdom in order to study English. He loved C.S. Lewis and dreamed of following in his footsteps. The idea was not totally farfetched since Nathan was actually an excellent writer. He just wasn't good at pushing himself to produce what was necessary to please his teachers.

Meanwhile, Nathan was confident that he could quickly find work that he enjoyed, or at least did not hate. He was wrong. After a few weeks, he went to a youth centre where help was offered in finding work. He was given a job washing dishes and although he did not like it, he decided that he would stick it out until he found something better. I was proud of him for that decision, but in the end it came to nothing. They let him go, telling him that he was too slow. So he tried some factory work, which he also hated, and they let him go for the same reason. Again I encouraged him to go to college, but he was not open to it.

I was praying more and more for Nathan. I longed for him to find a job that he could do reasonably well. I had no idea what that would be but I was sure that God knew, and that he would open the right doors for Nathan. Abigail had always fared much better when she looked for work, although she was only looking for part-time work. She communicated well and came across as a competent young lady, willing to work hard. Consequently she was offered most of the jobs she went after, and whatever position she received she did very well at. This did not encourage her brother.

Mike and I had diligently searched for work as well, in our respective fields. Mike worked for a firm that rented out video and television equipment, and he had the responsibility of keeping the equipment in running order. I was looking for work as a math teacher, and I was surprised at how hard that was. I worked for a few years in a tutoring facility on a part-time basis, and then slowly made my way into the public schools. Initially I worked in an adult education school, but since students typically enrolled one semester at a time, they couldn't predict how many teachers they would need and the work was inconsistent. I turned to the school board and tried to find temporary positions in different schools, replacing a teacher who was off for a period of time. Slowly I was gaining experience, with the hope that eventually I would find a permanent position in a high school not too far from where we lived.

Chapter 9: Finding employment is easy, right?

When Nathan did find a job, cutting huge beams with some filthy machine, he found that he really hated it. He was given the afternoon shift, and would come home from work exhausted and dirty. He wondered what the point of working was if you are too tired afterwards to enjoy a social life. He quit before long.

Living with Nathan was becoming increasingly challenging. He would usually stay out with his friends until the early hours of the morning and then sleep in until mid-day. He did nothing to help around the house and very little to find further work. When Mike and I were out of the house he would turn his music up loud, prompting the neighbours to call the police on more than one occasion. It was particularly hard on Abigail, to be at home with a brother who insisted on having his music as loud as he pleased. She would ask him politely to turn it down, but he refused. She even tried being *impolite*, but it was all water off a duck's back—Nathan did not seem to care about anyone except himself.

One particular meal time sticks out in my mind. Mike and I were trying to help Nathan understand that he had responsibilities both at home and in the community. In one breath he made it clear that he did not care one little bit what we thought he should be doing, and then he informed us what he wanted us to buy him for his birthday. I burst out laughing. Most of the time laughter was the last thing on my mind.

During that season I was averaging four hours a day just praying for Nathan. I would take a walk and spend the whole time crying out to God for a solution. How could we help him to find his way? I pleaded with God for an answer. I talked with a friend who had a business and asked him to consider taking Nathan on, but he had no vacancies. I searched for job openings that Nathan might like, and he even went on some interviews, but nothing came together for him. Finally, one day as I was driving home I saw Nathan walking along with a heavy kit bag, the kind of canvas bag that soldiers used to pack their belongings in—he was obviously moving out. I was both relieved and concerned.

If God would only show me what to do, I would do it. Why did it feel like he was not answering my prayers?

Whether God had turned his back on us or not, Nathan certainly had. We had given so much to him, not just possessions or provision, but hours of prayer and searching for a solution to his problems. How could he turn away so angry from us, when I had tried to help him with everything I had? It felt incredibly unfair.

Shortly after that, he turned away from the church also. Nathan had joined a church plant out of the Vineyard, a youth church, meeting in a coffee shop. The pastor, Brad, had spent a lot of time talking with Nathan, often into the early hours of the morning. Nathan had loved his pastor and spent many hours with him and his family. But now he was rejecting Brad and his church too. He felt that everyone had let him down. I was blessed that many continued to try and help him, however unsuccessful they may have been. Nathan was now living on welfare and had managed to find a small apartment. Unfortunately, welfare was enough to either pay his rent or buy food, but not both. I would go round to his apartment and bring him boxes of food. There were also soup kitchens in the area, and the church would sometimes provide him with food too. But still Nathan could not find work. He had been doing all the right things, but there really seemed to be nothing out there for him. A friend insisted that there were always jobs available

Chapter 9: Finding employment is easy, right?

if you were willing to try hard enough, especially in sales. That may have been true, but Nathan would not have been a very good salesman.

Nathan made some new friends at that time. Mostly they were young people like him who were also struggling to find suitable work. The Premier of Ontario (like the governor of a US state) had introduced the idea of giving every unemployed person work experience, while paying them welfare. I considered this to be wonderful for Nathan because so many interviews that he went on asked about his work experience, which was pretty much non-existent. The unions complained about it though, saying that it took people's jobs away by having someone do the work without pay. They had a good point, but it was so hard for inexperienced young people to find something they were capable of actually doing.

As Nathan was having so little success, I again suggested that he take something at college. Mike and I were more than willing to help him financially if he should have chosen to take a course that would better prepare him for the workforce. Again he refused to consider this as a viable option. He was rather enjoying his lifestyle, it turned out. In his own apartment there was no one to insist that he get up at a reasonable hour in the morning, no one to tell him to help with chores, no one pushing him to do anything that he did not want to do. In fact, he would spend hours lying in the bath, warming the water up every twenty minutes or so. Then he would visit a soup kitchen for lunch or cook some of the food I had brought him, and then go and hang out with his friends. Initially he paid his rent regularly and lived off the charity of others for food. When there were a few other things that he needed to purchase, he decided to take a break from paying rent, and he was quickly evicted.

I was there to help him move out, along with one of his friends from church. We packed so many things in boxes, and moved most of them to our garage. We were not able to move all of his furniture, so his landlord simply tossed it out of the window into the back yard, smashing everything. Nathan found some friends to move in with. Not all of Nathan's new friends were honest people. One young man asked Nathan to cash a cheque for him, since the man himself did not have a bank account. The young man gave Nathan an envelope, and told him it contained the cheque. Nathan dutifully deposited it, and withdrew two hundred dollars in cash and gave it to his new friend. Later it became clear that the envelope was empty. The police came to our home looking for Nathan, explaining what had happened. Nathan had already informed me about what had happened, and thankfully, they seemed to believe his story. Nathan never used his bank account again. He had learned the hard way that not all of his new friends were to be trusted.

Some of Nathan's new friends were also drug addicts. Nathan enjoyed marijuana himself, and he justified it by saying it wasn't as bad as the heroin his friends were using. Spending money on pot was probably where his rent money had gone, but he insisted that he needed to have some joy in his life. We would often invite our son round for a meal, and once he brought one of his new friends, whom he described as a 'cokehead.' He later apologised for bringing him to our home, concerned that he might come back and try to steal something. Fortunately, that never happened.

Other times Nathan would simply turn up, and inform us that he had not eaten for a day or more. I continued to pray long and hard for a breakthrough in his life, but it honestly felt like God was not hearing me.

Chapter 9: Finding employment is easy, right?

Eventually Nathan asked to move home again. His new friends had thrown him out of the apartment. He had used up all his favours with other friends and had also spent a couple of nights in a homeless shelter. There he made the mistake of taking his boots off before he went to sleep. In the morning his relatively new Doc Martens had been replaced with a pair of very old, worn shoes. He simply had nowhere else to turn to but us.

We agreed to his return as long as he accepted our terms: no drugs in the house, and he had to get up every morning and look for work. With no other option open to him, Nathan concurred. It was not long, however, before the fights started again. He saw no point looking for work because there was nothing out there. And when a job he was interested in did become available, they were not going to hire someone like him. He had applied for a position at the local cinema, but they made it clear that they preferred to hire younger people, because they did not have to pay them as much. Nathan was only nineteen himself, but they would have had to pay him more than someone who was under eighteen.

I prayed so many hours for him to find work that he could stick with. I felt that Nathan needed to feel useful, that he could actually do a job. For whatever reason, my prayers never appeared to be answered. Nathan took his frustration out on us and desperately looked for a way out. He was depressed and angry. He felt that his family had failed him. That God had failed him. That the church had failed him. He needed to get away. Nathan decided that it would be easier to find work on the other side of Canada and made plans to leave. We had another argument, Nathan walked out of the house, and I never saw him again.

Loving Nathan

CHAPTER 10: NATHAN'S LAST CHAPTER

I was heartbroken when Nathan left home again. Why did he have to travel thousands of miles away from both his natural family and his church family? I was also emotionally exhausted. I had invested so much into Nathan over the years. I had prayed for hours on end, although I wavered between trusting that God was hearing me and wondering why I was not seeing any change. I had connected with several friends and acquaintances who had their own businesses and tried to persuade them to hire him. I tried talking to people who might need someone to do odd jobs around their homes. I walked into stores and asked if they were hiring. I encouraged him. I prayed for him. I gave him everything I could think of, I really tried. But I seemed unable to help him. How could God say that he loved me and yet he was leaving me to flounder in this relationship with my son?

Mike was not faring much better than I. He could see that I was running around like a chicken with my head cut off, and he simply felt helpless. He was struggling with his own feelings of inadequacy, and fell into depression. Despite this, he managed to continue functioning as a responsible husband and father to our two daughters.

Abigail was not doing well in her relationship with Nathan. She could see that he was behaving irresponsibly and that he was unfairly blaming his parents, and she was angry at him for it. He was not kind towards her either. Nathan was in his own little world, and although he cared a lot for his friends, he did not show any love or consideration towards his family.

One person in the family who still thought that Nathan was something special was his little sister, Hannah. She was just seven and was fairly oblivious to his selfish, and sometimes downright inappropriate behaviour. Once he told her how he could get an erection by wearing a kilt and no underwear, and then rubbing up next to certain young ladies. I'm glad that she didn't understand what he was talking about, she was just happy that he would seek her out to spend time together. Sadly, we felt it best to subtly try and keep them from being alone together for any length of time.

I desperately wanted to help my son come to a place of peace, to find purpose and meaning, work and friendships where he could truly thrive. At the same time, I often found myself feeling very angry with him because he did not seem willing to recognise his own responsibilities in any situation. Despite his self-centred attitude and his unwillingness to help in any way at home, we all still loved him and wanted the best for him, so this was a very difficult time for everyone. I personally struggled to experience God's love at this time, wondering why heaven seemed deaf to my prayers. I kept telling myself that what I was experiencing did not alter the truth of who God is, that he is a God who loves and cares for all his children. With somewhat floundering faith I was able to acknowledge that God did indeed still love both my son and myself.

It took Nathan just three days to hitchhike across Canada. He emailed me from an internet café to let us know that he had arrived safely. It was encouraging to know that he was making the effort to stay in touch, and we were relieved to know that he had safely travelled such a long distance. It gave me courage that he knew we still cared deeply about him.

Apparently, a large number of young people were

Chapter 10: Nathan's Last Chapter

living on the streets in Vancouver and Nathan quickly made some new acquaintances. He even found an old friend from Vineyard days who had moved across the country and would volunteer at one of the many soup kitchens. Vancouver didn't impress Nathan very much, so he quickly found a way to travel across the water to Victoria. There he made some new friends, including one young lady who became his girlfriend. He was absolutely smitten with Brianna, and informed us that God had provided him with a 'fair maiden.' I found it interesting that he considered her a gift from God, since he had so strongly rejected the church. Actually, he had previously informed me that although he believed the church had let him down, he still believed in God. I guess after everything else he still had some kind of relationship with the Lord.

Nathan and Brianna, together with some other friends, managed to find an apartment together. They had been sleeping outside but as the weather became colder this was less and less fun. When the waiting period had passed for Nathan to claim welfare, he did so. Now he was required to look for work again, and he took it quite seriously this time. Nathan loved books and working in a bookstore seemed like an appropriate place for him. He applied to work in a local bookstore, and I believe he could have done well there, but they did not hire him. Meanwhile Nathan and Brianna were busking in the streets in order to make enough money to eat. Nathan was now taller than his father, a full six foot six inches, and he was very thin. The restaurant they liked to frequent seemed to take pity on him and he would often receive a larger portion than his friends.

In some ways Nathan was much happier now, even though he still could not find a job. He and his friends did some occasional work helping people move things for a bit of extra cash. He loved Brianna, yet he was still struggling with his identity. When he had lived with us Nathan had sometimes worn a dress. We had never done anything to stop this, although when he was still at school we had denied him the option of wearing black nail polish since we wanted to protect him from bullies. In British Columbia, Nathan again wore a dress on occasion. At the same time, he enjoyed his relationship with Brianna, and none of his friends expressed any concern with his unusual behaviour.

My walk with God was improving again. Nathan was safe and he was communicating with us. Without the problem staring me in the face every day, I found that I was no longer praying for Nathan hour after hour. I still prayed for him daily but not to the extent I had previously. I was trusting him into God's hands and was confident that God was going to bring him back to me as a more content young man.

Nathan would email every few weeks, and at Christmas we even received a phone call. Social Services had given out phone cards as Christmas gifts, and we were so thrilled to hear from him. He was obviously still very angry with the church in general and not willing to admit any responsibility for the falling out. We found out later that he had said some negative things about Brad, his pastor, and became angry when challenged on them. Some of the other young folks had visited Nathan and he thought they had come just to hang out. In fact, they had come to confront him for his behaviour so he threw them out. He wanted nothing to do with the church after that. Abigail challenged him on some of the harsh things he was saying about the church, but Mike and I did our best to keep the conversation positive. Nonetheless, we were so happy to have a pleasant conversation with him, especially after he had left with some very angry words.

In May of that year Nathan had the opportunity to go camping with Brianna and another friend. He was really enjoying his new relationships, although something was

Chapter 10: Nathan's Last Chapter

obviously bothering him. They hitchhiked out of the city into the nearby forest, and found a spot to put up their tents close to a river. Nathan was very agitated and he was saying things that did not make sense to them, like the stars not lining up properly. Nothing they could say to him seemed to help. Eventually he took off in order to walk by himself. The two girls wanted to give him the opportunity to work out whatever it was that was bothering him, and hoped the walk would do him good. When it grew dark and Nathan had not returned, the girls became anxious. They walked a little distance from the tents, calling his name, but when they received no response they returned to where they had set up, hoping that he would soon return. They did not sleep at all during the night and were very concerned as to what might have happened to him.

As soon as it was light they went looking for him again, and then they tried calling their mutual friends in Victoria to see if he had returned there. Since he had been so agitated the night before they wondered if he had simply hitchhiked back to where they lived. Nobody they called had seen or heard from him, so they decided to call the police. The police made some inquiries, and apparently he *had* attempted to hitch a ride, though in the dark he must have looked quite scary and no one stopped to pick him up.

The following day the police found his body eight kilometers further down the river. He had drowned. The coroner had to ask the question of whether he had deliberately entered the river. He had acted as if he were tormented before he disappeared and it would have made sense if perhaps he had chosen to end his life. There were scratches on his hands, which indicated that even if he had jumped into the river, he had tried to pull himself out again.

When we eventually spoke with the police in Victoria ourselves they said that Nathan would have drowned relatively quickly. The water was fast and furious due to the snow melting in the mountains and running down into the river. The water was also very cold, and they expected that he would not have lasted more than ten minutes before he would have had to give up.

What was going through his mind in those last moments? Did he call out to the God whom he had once considered a friend? Did he realise that he was about to enter eternity? Was he terrified? I can only guess. I know I would have been. Some friends have encouraged me to believe that Nathan probably understood enough of what was happening, and knew enough to call out again to the Lord. That is indeed likely, but we will not know for sure until we too enter eternity.

I have been over Nathan's last few minutes so many times in my mind. He would have been so cold, and so sad. Had he wanted to die and then changed his mind? Did he slip in while trying to relieve himself? There was so much pain in his short life, and so much more as he died. The marks on Nathan's hands indicated that he fought hard pull himself out of the river. It hurts me so much that Nathan tried and God did not provide the means for him to actually get free.

CHAPTER 11: IT'S OVER

Had God let me down? I had felt that God was hearing my prayers. I also expected that if Nathan was in a dangerous situation then God would speak to me so I could pray. If anyone had suggested to me that my son was going to die I would have laughed at them and told them that God was looking after him. I had faith for that. The police had left, Abigail had returned home, and gone to bed, our pastor had left, and Mike and I just sat there in the stillness. I sensed something of Nathan in those quiet moments. I sensed him weeping. Not an agonized weeping as if he were being sent away from the presence of God, but rather an anguished weeping as if he had failed to do all that he was supposed to do. I sensed a deep burden that he had not shared the Lord with the person he loved most, Brianna. I sensed a great sadness that he had painted for himself such a negative picture of the Lord. The feeling did not last long, but it felt very real. I believe God peeled back the layers of heaven and earth, and space and time, for one gracious moment so I could see into the heart of my son whom I had spent so many years trying to understand.

We did go to church the next day. I cried through most of the worship, but we were there. Many friends cried with us. There was emotional support for each of us, and in the next couple of weeks support came practically as well. I barely ate anything for three days, food was like dust in my food. Eventually I began to enjoy the different meals that various friends provided for us. Mike organised the visitation and the funeral. Through an incredibly generous gift from the school where I was working at the time, we were able to fly Nathan's body back from British Columbia.. Many others helped us financially as well, as we had no savings to fall back on. It is shocking how much it costs to bring a body across the country, and then to have a funeral, and cremation. My mother flew in from England to support us too, even though she was not particularly well herself. She found it so difficult seeing Nathan in the coffin, and remarked that he looked a lot like her husband when he died.

Some of Nathan's friends from when he attended school were at the funeral, and some friends from church. And our own friends came too, to stand with us at this difficult time. Several spoke positively of Nathan's friendship, and Mike and I both shared too, although I found it hard to read what I had prepared since I was crying so much. Our pastor had paid for refreshments to be served after the funeral, and we had the opportunity to speak with many who had travelled quite a distance to share in this sad day.

And finally it was over.

It was helpful to have work to busy myself with during those first few weeks after the funeral, and teaching is a very demanding job. My colleagues were very supportive and somehow life managed to go on. In the summer, Mike, Hannah and I made the journey to Victoria to meet with some of Nathan's friends and to scatter his ashes in Stanley Park. It felt so wrong arriving at Vancouver Airport to find he was not there to greet us. But it was important that we had made this journey, even though it was not going to be easy. The same family from our Vineyard church who had originally connected with Nathan at the soup kitchen kindly offered us a place to stay. We visited Nathan's friends, and had a short ceremony with them. Somehow I kept hoping that God would resurrect him whilst we still had his ashes, but once they were gone so were my hopes. We visited the restaurant that had been so generous to Nathan, and we walked where he had walked. We walked without him, and it was simply, achingly, incredibly sad.

Victoria is a beautiful city, and everyone was so kind to us, but I was relieved to depart. I was glad we went, but I never want to go again. Victoria is Nathan's city, and because I cannot share it with him, I do not want to go there again.

We did experience God's love in those hard days, weeks and months after Nathan's death, in a tangible way, through the practical help and generosity of friends and family. Sometimes the only way that we can receive love from God is through other people, and we were frequently on the receiving end in those weeks and months. One couple that we had only known for a few months drove over to our house and gave us a thousand dollars towards the expense of Nathan's funeral. Other friends, who did not have that kind of money to spare, blessed us immensely with gifts of fifty dollars, or a hundred, or ten. We did not ask for anything, but people understood that the last thing we needed to worry about at this time was where the necessary finances would come from. The kindness of Nathan's friends in Victoria we greatly appreciated, and we received it as another blessing from the Lord. It would have been so much better, however, if Nathan could have introduced us to his friends himself. I felt so let down by God. This is not what I had prayed for. I could not understand what had gone wrong, and why God had not intervened.

CHAPTER 12: DARKNESS

This was the hardest time of my life. Everything around me felt like darkness. Sometimes there would be a small glimmer of light, like when you are in a darkened room and a door opens somewhere far off. As I moved towards the light, however, it was as if the door closed again and everything would become totally dark once more.

Initially I thought about Nathan every day, dreamed about him every night. And after the dream I would wake up and go through the reality of his drowning yet again. After a while I started using the authority that I have in Jesus' wonderful name to bind the enemy before I went to sleep at night. When I remembered to do that, I did not dream about Nathan, and when I forgot to take authority over the enemy, I did dream about him. This continued for several months. I know some people like to dream about their loved one who died because it keeps up a connection. In my case the dreams were different every time, though they often ended up with Nathan dying. Sometimes he would die in a fight, or a road accident, or a fire in his home. I would awake confused, knowing that he did not die like that, and then wonder, for a while, if he was actually dead at all. And after a few minutes the truth would once again make its way to my conscious brain: he had drowned, he was dead. Yes, the enemy was definitely using my dreams to torment me, and I was so glad that the Lord had given us, his children, authority over the devil and his schemes.

Despite using the name of Jesus to stop some of my daily torment, I was ready to give up on my relationship with God. I still prayed, but my prayer times were filled with profanity and anger. I read the Bible, although I avoided the New Testament. There was not a doubt in my mind that God could have protected Nathan from drowning, but for whatever reason he had not. Why read stories in the Bible where God had healed people, provided miraculously for people and loved on them in the way I wished he had loved on me? Before Nathan had hitchhiked across the country, I had been praying an average of four hours a day for him. I worked only part time, and was desperate for the Lord to strongly intervene in his life. Then when he left, I did not know what he was doing, whether he was looking for work, finding food, living on the streets or in an apartment, or anything like that, I had no real idea what I should be praying for. So my main prayer became that he would know that Father God loved him. I prayed over and over again that he would come to experience the love of God for himself. Drowning and going to be with the Lord was not how I envisioned my prayers being answered. Basically I felt that God had totally failed to answer my prayers. And consequently I was ready to call it quits, no more praying.
I was still going through the motions of Christianity. I continued to regularly attend church, to pray every day and to read my Bible every day. This was all so much a part of who I was that I simply could not stop. The truth was that I have experienced God in my life in so many tangible ways that I could not now choose to simply not believe in him. Instead I was just very, very angry at him, and wanted to push him away. At the same time, I did

Chapter 12: Darkness

long for him to draw close to me, but the pain of losing my son seemed to put a huge wedge between Father God and myself. This brought even more pain for me, in that not only had I lost my son, but I seemed to have lost my relationship with God as well.

I did consider what other options might be available for me. Getting drunk held some appeal, but the thought of a hangover afterwards did not. Alcohol would definitely dull the pain for a while, but it would not bring a permanent solution, so I rejected that idea. I considered drugs, although I had no idea where to get them from. The thought of my two remaining children having to deal with a mother who took drugs helped me to reject that option. So then I tried looking at different religions and belief systems. The problem was that no matter what people believed or embraced in their lives, they still could not avoid death. Since my anger with God was based on the death of my son, none of the other belief systems had any more to offer me than Christianity.

If it's not clear already, I think very logically. I have been a math teacher for many years, so I suppose it makes sense that I value logic as a way of working things out. However, simply recognising that there was no real competition for Christianity didn't really help me very much. Yes, I had strongly entrenched habits of prayer, and of reading my Bible, and I belonged to and continued to attend a local fellowship of believers, but God felt a million miles away. What was I to do? Nathan was not coming back, the pain would not go away, and I felt stuck. Over the years I have helped many Christians as they struggled with their individual situations. Mike and I have led small groups both in the local church and in YWAM. We have been responsible to help and encourage others as they struggled with the death of a loved one, or the divorce of their parents. I have helped disciple many young women and counselled them after they have been abused or rejected. I have prayed for deliverance for those who were struggling with demonic oppression, suicidal thoughts or strong desires to self-harm. Now I needed to remind myself of some of the tools I had used to help others. There was one illustration in particular which I had found quite helpful among Christians going through very difficult times.

Imagine yourself in a large room. You need to get out of this room. Between you and the door are a great many tables and chairs, but you can see your way to the exit clearly enough. Suddenly, the light goes out, and you are plunged into total darkness. You have three choices:

- Panic, forget the way that you previously knew was there, and crash into tables and chairs all over the place;
- Refuse to move at all, stay right where you are;
- Pursue the peace you had when the lights were on, remain calm, and continue walking in the direction that you knew to be correct just a few moments before.

I had shared this illustration on several different occasions in the past, and now I was facing it myself. Everything around me was darkness. Yet not so long ago I was sure of God's love, and of how I should live my life. All I needed to do now was to continue in what I had been so sure of earlier. And that is what I chose to do.

It would be nice if I could say that everything quickly returned to normal in my life and in my walk with the Lord, but I knew that things would never be the same. To this day I still have some huge questions that largely remain unanswered. The biggest one is why didn't God

Chapter 12: Darkness

answer my prayers? Reconciling the goodness of God with God's seeming refusal to answer my prayers was difficult. My pastor did his best to come alongside Mike and I and offer some guidance. He rephrased my question like this, *"Why were our prayers not enough?"* This allowed room for me to humbly acknowledge that I don't understand all things, while still asking God for an answer. It would have been easy for someone to say that God knew what was best for Nathan, or that Nathan was in a better place now. That was not what I had been praying for, so it would have simply angered me. At the same time I had to recognise that Nathan made his own choices and ultimately I do not understand the ways of God.

It was a great relief that no one tried to tell me how I should act at this point. I was given freedom to express freely to God all that I needed to. I especially appreciated that my pastor did not try to come up with any answers himself. He did not offer any pat answers or any platitudes. Ed even tolerated me when I found an old t-shirt with the word "LOSER" in bold words on the front. On the back, was the Scripture *"Whoever loses his life for the sake of the gospel will find it."* This made it safe enough to wear to church, but the truth was I did feel like a loser. I had lost my son!

Feeling like a loser was new for me. Previous to losing Nathan I had felt strong in my walk with the Lord. I had confidence that I could hear from God, and was confident that I had things to share with others. I have felt that my main gifting in the body of Christ was as a teacher of the Word, and I had actively looked for opportunities to share some of the things that the Lord had taught me over the years.

In the various times that I have taught others, in discipleship training schools, youth groups, and sometimes churches, one of my topics has often been intercession. I believe in prayer. I believe it makes a difference. In fact, I believe that God has, to a certain extent, restricted himself to the prayers of his people.

I have heard incredible prayers and I have seen incredible answers to prayer. Despite my own tragedy, I cannot deny the power of prayer.

In 1989 I joined with thousands of people praying for Eastern Europe's freedom from Communism. Shortly after the Berlin Wall came down, our whole family had the privilege of participating in an outreach in Czechoslovakia. We were part of a team from the YWAM base in Amsterdam, a team made up of staff and their families. Nathan and Abigail were 12 and 11 and little Hannah was just four months old.

Four years prior to the outreach, a young man in Czechoslovakia had spoken into the air, *"God, if you exist, show yourself to me."* Three years later he had a dream, and in that dream he saw a group of people arrive in his city and place a huge mat in Wenceslas Square. Then he saw a young man stand up and speak, and although he could not hear what this person said, he understood that he was talking about God. This was a very clear dream, and he held it in his heart for another year. Then we came to Prague and placed a huge mat in Wenceslas Square! The children performed a short presentation, which Nathan and Abigail were a part of. Then we adults performed a mime story of the gospel. The young man who had had the dream happened to be in the Square that day, and he stopped to watch, wondering if this had anything to do with what he had seen in his dream. When someone stood up to share the gospel the young man was absolutely amazed. He recognised the man from his dream!

As soon as the preaching drew to a conclusion, and

Chapter 12: Darkness

the invitation was given to accept Jesus, the young man who had asked God to reveal himself to him rushed to the side of our big mat and knelt in commitment to the Lord. Hundreds of others responded as well. Many others who had gathered to watch weren't yet ready to make a commitment, but neither were they about to walk away. So the rest of us paired up to pray for those who were interested in what we had to say. I personally made an effort to always include a young person with me when I prayed. My desire was that the young folks would also experience the Holy Spirit moving through them to touch people. There were often many locals who spoke English who were willing to translate for us. As we prayed for the different people they would often sense something of God's presence themselves. I remember a couple of Czech girls who spoke good English, and one of them had a headache. They were skeptical when we offered to pray but gave us permission anyway. Afterwards they were both blown away because not only was the headache gone, but they had felt that God was present to them. This was a most incredible experience, for Mike and I and also for Nathan and Abigail. For the first time we experienced the power of God in a tangible way. We saw healings, and we saw many, many people, young and old, commit their lives to the Lord.

I have experienced other answers to prayer as well. I have often been given by the Lord a word of knowledge, knowing something about a person that they have not informed me of, in order that I may pray more effectively for that person. For example, when I was praying for one young man the Lord had me ask him if he had participated in certain occult practices. He wondered how I knew, and quickly repented of all that he had done. He soon had a wonderful breakthrough in his marriage, as he gave up control of his wife.

Occasionally I have also prophesied over people, including informing a wonderful Christian in my home church that God wanted to take his ministry much further afield. The man was incredulous at the time, but has since ministered in many different nations. Other prophetic words that I have given to people were perhaps not so exciting, but they often brought hope and encouragement. I say all this not to boast, for it is the grace of God that he chooses to use me at all, but to explain that I had experienced some exciting things with God, and I had expectations for what he would do for my son. Not least, I totally believed that if Nathan was in a very difficult situation, then God would let me know, and I would pray into whatever was going on with him, and Nathan would be protected. But God did not put Nathan on my heart when he was camping by the river, obviously upset and by the sounds of it, tormented.

Through all these difficult times, God helped me to continue in my responsibilities as a mother to my other two children. Abigail had some support from her boyfriend at the time, and his mother even came with him to Nathan's funeral. Unfortunately the relationship did not last much longer after this, and Abigail then had her own feelings of hurt and rejection to deal with. Mike and I tried to support her as much as possible after Nathan died, but really I think she supported us more. Abigail did not seem to mourn the death of her brother for long. I assumed it was because they were not close when he died, but the truth was she simply pushed it all down inside her. When she met Jon, who is now her husband, things came to the surface gradually. With his support, and ours when we had the opportunity, she too began to slowly deal with Nathan's death.

Chapter 12: Darkness

Hannah was devastated to lose her big brother. She had problems at school, and was very angry at God. She had loved swimming up until then, but has mostly kept away from the water ever since. I prayed for her frequently as well, probably more than I did for Abigail. I once mentioned to my pastor that I thought Abigail would do brilliantly in life whether or not I prayed for her! Of course, there are times when we *all* need more prayer support and I have learned to pray more and more for both of my daughters. And I still have the same expectation, that if either of them are particularly in need and I am unaware of it, the Lord will speak to me to intercede on their behalf.

In case you think that makes me crazy, I shall share one final story to vindicate my belief in prayer. I was recently on vacation with my husband in Costa Rica, where I was working on this manuscript. Although I had my cell phone with me, I kept it in flight mode all the time because I did not want to receive any texts from friends who were unaware that I was out of the country. It was possible to pay for Wifi at the resort where we were staying, but I was in vacation mode, and had not made the effort to find out how. One morning I suddenly felt a strong burden to pray for Hannah. She has some health issues, but everything was fine the day that we left Canada. I walked up and down the beach, praying hard for my daughter. I even turned flight mode off on my cell phone, in case she had sent me a message, but there was nothing. So I continued to pray for about an hour until I felt the burden ease.

As soon as we had landed back in Toronto I texted my daughter, asking her if everything was okay, explaining also that I had been led to pray hard for her the previous morning. Within a couple of minutes, she called, and explained a particular problem that she had encountered with her health that had made her very anxious, and she feared, with good reason, that something might happen during a performance that she was taking part in. She had already participated in two performances the previous evening and had one more that night. She was so encouraged that the Lord had put her on my heart to pray the day before, and asked that her father and I pray again that night.

The very thing that I believed would occur when Nathan was having problems, occurred for Hannah. I would have prayed very hard if God had given me a burden to pray for my son, but for some reason he did not.

Why were my prayers insufficient as far as Nathan was concerned? Why did God not open the doors for Nathan to find meaningful work here in Cambridge? Why did God not heal Nathan, help him more with his struggles? I do not know, and I do not think I will know this side of eternity. Can I trust God without knowing all the answers?

It is important for me to consider what I do know, rather than spending too much time on my unanswered questions. I do know that God is love. I have read the Scriptures over and over, and they clearly present God as a God of love. There are so many places I could quote from, but the first epistle of John is an excellent place to go to:

> "Whoever does not love does not know God, because God is love. This is how God showed his love among us: He sent his one and only Son into the world that we might live through him. This is love: not that we loved God, but that he loved us

and sent his Son as an atoning sacrifice for our sins. Dear friends, since God so loved us, we also ought to love one another. No one has ever seen God; but if we love one another, God lives in us and his love is made complete in us. This is how we know that we live in him and he in us: He has given us of his Spirit. And we have seen and testify that the Father has sent his Son to be the Savior of the world. If anyone acknowledges that Jesus is the Son of God, God lives in them and they in God. And so we know and rely on the love God has for us. God is love. Whoever lives in love lives in God, and God in them." (1 John 4: 8-16)

The writer of this epistle is not named, and it has been debated since the second century as to whether the apostle John wrote it, along with the gospel bearing his name and The Revelation, or even any of them. In those days it was not important to have an actual name to each book, not least because they were not written in order to be added into the Bible. They were written to encourage different groups, and it was only later that they came to be seen to have value far beyond their original intention. What is known about this epistle is that it was written during a time of difficulty. There was persecution, some false teaching that detracted from the glory of Christ, and many Christians were not experiencing all that Christ had to offer. My point is that it is easy to say that God is love when everything is going right in our lives. Clearly at the time in history that this was written, all was not well. Hence, I can read this book and understand that "God is love" does not mean everything will go the way I want it to. But God is faithful, and we can know that God is love through our relationship with him. That has been so important for me to come to understand.

    I do believe that God is merciful and kind, and that he cares deeply about all that happens to me. It may not have felt like that was true during and after my struggles with Nathan, but I regularly remind myself that my personal experiences do not alter the truth of who God is. And as you will see, I have experienced something of the mercy of God with my daughter Hannah.

CHAPTER 13: HANNAH

Children are a blessing from the Lord! If we ever tried to count or measure our blessings, I think we would miss noticing most of them. His love for us is generous and constant, and I was incredibly blessed to give birth to three children.

We had always assumed that two children would be enough for us. Rather than go through the expense of purchasing contraceptives over a long period of time, we decided that Mike would just get a vasectomy. All went well, until Nathan and Abigail grew a little older. Once they were no longer wanting to sit on our laps when we watched TV, I started to think that I would like to have another child. Mike has always been very easy going, and I think the idea of becoming a father again also appealed to him, so he made enquiries about a reversal operation. The procedure did not take long. When it came time for Mike's follow-up appointment to ensure that everything had been successfully returned to normal, I called the doctor and canceled it. There was no need for a follow-up. I was already pregnant.

Hannah was born in a little hospital on the outskirts of Amsterdam. It was quite a different experience from my first two births, in the cultural comfort of my own country. When the contractions were painful I asked for drugs. The doctor insisted that Dutch women were strong and did not need drugs in order to bring a child into the world. *"I'm not Dutch, I'm English!"* I insisted, but the doctor only laughed. Fortunately, it was not too long after that that Hannah came into the world. Hannah was one year old when we moved to Canada. She loved her brother, Nathan, and his death was devastating for her as an 11 year old. In the aftermath of his death she lashed out at many people, including her teachers. One day she ran away from school, and her teacher had to leave her class with the principal while she went out in her car to look for her. We found Hannah before her teacher did, since she had gone to see Brad, who had been Nathan's pastor. He was very kind to her, and so was her teacher, and she returned to school the next day. Those were difficult times for her, but she managed to get through school more positively than Nathan did.

After graduating, Hannah was not sure what she wanted to do with her life. She had applied to a couple of universities, and was accepted but did not feel ready for a university education. Instead she chose to go to Conestoga College to study Broadcasting. There were parts of the course that she enjoyed, and parts that she considered a waste of time, but she persevered and graduated two years later. One summer during her course, Mike found an ad for a video person at a Christian camp in Arnes, an hour north of Winnipeg. Hannah applied, got the position, and spent her summer in Manitoba. Since it was such a positive experience for her, the following year she decided to go to the camp again, this time as a counsellor.

It was a beautiful summers' day. Mike had recently changed from working with a small company renting out equipment, to working at the University of Waterloo. He had been delivering equipment there on occasion, and had

Chapter 13: Hannah

built a relationship with some of the staff there. When a job became available for an electronic technologist, they let Mike know about it, and when he applied he was quickly hired. I also had now obtained a permanent teaching position with the Separate School Board, at a high school in Guelph. Since I was a teacher I had the summers off, something I really appreciated. Mike had left for work and I was slowly beginning my day at home. There had been a phone call the night before, after we had gone to bed. By the time we made it to the phone the person trying to call us had given up. They did not leave a message and we wondered who it could have been, but then thought no more about it. Then the phone rang in the morning. I answered with my normal cheery response. It was a neurologist in the ER in a hospital in Winnipeg. He had phoned to tell me Hannah was in the hospital.

    A couple of days earlier, Hannah had felt unwell, with a bad headache. After spending the day in the infirmary at the camp, she was not getting any better, and nothing they tried was able to improve the pain. The nurse decided to take Hannah to the hospital in Gimli. The doctor saw her, and was confident that she simply had the flu. As they were taking Hannah back to the car she collapsed. The doctor saw her again and realised that this was probably not the flu after all and arranged for an ambulance to send her to the much larger hospital in Winnipeg. There she was given a CAT scan which revealed a blood clot in her brain. The emergency neurologist woke the lead neurologist up, and he called an MRI technician into work in the middle of the night. They discovered that Hannah was also bleeding in her brain. Her condition was very bleak. The doctor was calling us to basically tell us that if we wanted to see our daughter while she was still alive, we needed to get on a plane as soon as possible!

I had already called Mike, and he was on his way home from work. Then I called Abigail, who was now living on the outskirts of Toronto with Jon, her husband, and one young child. She decided immediately that she was going to come too. Somehow I managed to book flights for Abigail, her husband, their daughter, Mike and I. We arranged to meet them at the airport, but before we left home the hospital in Winnipeg called to let us know that they could not wait until we arrived, they had to operate on Hannah immediately.

It is a fairly short flight from Toronto to Winnipeg, but it seemed agonizingly long that day. I was trying to pray, knowing that this situation could easily go very badly. I thought that God would be merciful, this time he *had* to save my child. I wondered what I could offer him, to persuade him to be merciful. Andrew McMillan says that fear makes bad theologians out of us and that was certainly true for me that day. I decided that having given Jesus my whole life there was nothing really left after that. But I cried out nonetheless; I could not bear the thought of losing another child!

As soon as we landed I looked around for the nearest phone and put in a call to the hospital. We were quickly informed that the operation was a success. Abigail was right next to me and we fell weeping into each other's arms. We were so relieved. Jon was a little way off with their daughter, and looked over at us full of concern. Abigail quickly gave him a thumbs up, and we all felt just a little bit better. A friend of a friend picked us up from the airport and drove us straight to the hospital. Initially, only I was permitted into the ICU and I was directed to Hannah's bedside. The doctor who performed the surgery was right there with her, and she was beginning to wake

Chapter 13: Hannah

up. I said her name, but there was no reaction on Hannah's part. My heart sank. I am aware that after brain surgery there can be all sorts of consequences, and immediately I was concerned that Hannah would not know who I was. The doctor signaled to me to go to the other side of the bed, however, and this time when I said her name the response was very different. Hannah threw her arms around me crying. She was confused about what was going on, and was so relieved to have her mother there to support her.

I felt that God had been kind to me. I still had my daughter. And over the ensuing weeks and months we began to learn how close Hannah had actually come to death. If they had given her blood thinners when they discovered her blood clot, she would have bled to death since she was already bleeding in her brain. If they hadn't performed an MRI they wouldn't have known this. If the whole thing had happened in a different location, she would possibly not have received as good care as she had. This was a teaching hospital, and the surgeon was brilliant. We didn't realise how brilliant until we met another surgeon at McMaster Hospital a year later. After Hannah had been released from the hospital in Winnipeg she flew home with us to Cambridge, and was later given a follow-up appointment in Hamilton, the closest hospital location with a good neurology apartment. The chief surgeon there insisted that he be the person to see her because he had never seen anyone survive a brain bleed as bad as hers!

Although Hannah survived the ordeal, she developed some disabilities as a result of what happened. She has lost some of her peripheral vision, and consequently could not continue to drive. She did, after all, lose part of her brain in the operation. Six years after her surgery, she also developed epilepsy, but she is still alive and well today.

All of this begged the question from me, as to why God answered my prayers for Hannah and yet did not answer my prayers for Nathan. A part of me would be tempted to point out that a few days before she got sick Hannah rededicated her life to the Lord. Perhaps he protected her because of her act of faith. Another part of me remembers hearing a visiting preacher who, in 1988, was due to be on a Pan Am flight from Frankfurt to Detroit, which was blown out of the sky over Lockerbie, Scotland. At the last minute this preacher was changed to another flight, for no apparent reason, and because of that he did not die with the 259 passengers and crew who did. Yet he had a friend whose daughter was on the plane, and she loved God as well as he did. I also remember a young man from YWAM who was on his way to our base in Lausanne, and he died in the Swissair flight that crashed near Peggy's Cove, Nova Scotia. Clearly being dedicated to the Lord does not necessarily mean that God will protect you from a premature death.

I have wrestled with this question for years. I am a math teacher, I have to admit that I like formulas. For good or ill, there is not one that fits these situations. My prayers were not enough to see Nathan brought to complete health and freedom. I do not understand why. And although it did not take me long to realise that I still wanted to follow the Lord after Nathan's death, it took me a lot longer before I began to pray for anything as long and hard as I had done for my son. It was also several years before I wanted to really worship God again too. I am not sure that everyone thinks too much about what they are singing in praise and worship songs, but I personally pay very close attention to the words. I heard a song recently where the words declare that God will never let us down, and I struggle to sing that. It irks me that I feel this way still, and I have told the Lord that I trust him, and I acknowledge that he knows so much more than me, and yet I still feel let down. But I believe God understands that and does not hold it against me.

If I were to look at all the things, friendships and family that I possess, and consider all of them blessings from God, then I am indeed a very blessed person. We have our own home, my husband and I each have our own cars, we have a large television, several computers, our home is fully furnished, we have an above ground pool in the back garden. The list goes on. I have travelled quite extensively and I am aware that we in the West have so many more material possessions than those elsewhere. This begs the question—does God love people in the West more than those in second and third world countries? If we only judged God's love by material possessions, we might say yes. But I have observed that other parts of the world have a wealth of spirituality, community and family that makes them look blessed, and us not. The rain falls on the just and the unjust (Matthew 5:45).

In Romans 9:13 we hear it said *"Just as it is written: Jacob have I loved, but Esau I hated."* Yet Jacob had an awful time throughout most of his life. After stealing his brother's birthright he flees from his family in fear of his life. He then finds a woman he wants to marry, works for seven years in order to marry her, and on the wedding night discovers that they swapped her out for her sister. He ends up working another seven years and is repeatedly deceived and cheated. His beloved wife dies in childbirth and when he finally reconciles with his brother he discovers that his brother has lived a blessed life!

> Esau asked, "What's the meaning of all these flocks and herds I met?" "To find favor in your eyes, my lord," he said. But Esau said, "I already have plenty, my brother. Keep what you have for yourself." (Genesis 33:8-9)

Jacob buys land nearby, and then his favourite son is apparently killed by animals. At the end of his life he discovers his son lives, and he ends up meeting Pharaoh, the ruler of Egypt.

> And Jacob said to Pharaoh, "The years of my pilgrimage are a hundred and thirty. My years have been few and difficult, and they do not equal the years of the pilgrimage of my fathers." (Genesis 47:9)

And yet we are told in Romans that God loved Jacob and hated Esau?! Clearly there is something deeper happening under the surface. If my life is any witness to this, then the evidence of God's love is rarely what we expect it to be. What I do notice, when I look beyond the outward appearance, is that twice Jacob had incredible encounters with God. First, when he was running away from his brother, he stops for the night at a place called Bethel. God meets with him there, and reiterates the promises that were made to his father and grandfather before him saying that his descendants would be as plentiful as the dust of the earth, and that all people on earth would be blessed through him and his offspring (see Genesis 28:10-15). Then later, before his reconciliation with his brother, Jacob actually wrestles with God for a blessing, and God gives him a new name, Israel (see Genesis 32:22-32).

Chapter 13: Hannah

These two God encounters are what Jacob receives but Esau does not. Personally I would rather have an encounter with the Living God, the creator of the universe, than anything that money can buy. I do not understand all that God does or does not do, but it seems clear to me now that God's love is measured in relationship, rather than in material. I have experienced some wonderful times in my walk with God, times when I was so aware that God was with me. And because of these, perhaps more than anything else, I am convinced that I am loved by Him. I also believe it is the heart of a good Father for his children to be healthy and content. I have yet to fully live out the health part, but it seems clear to me from the New Testament, that Jesus, God's son, did not accept sickness as being normal. I continue to live in the tension between what I believe is true of God, and what I am experiencing in front of me. One of many things I have learned from the Catholics is the power in the Lord's Prayer: Thy kingdom come, thy will be done, on Earth as it is Heaven.

Of one thing I am certain—God loves me. I realise when I look back that despite my fear, my doubt and my confusion, this has never really been in question. He does not give me everything I want, but he has most definitely given me some wonderful things, including a wonderful family. I am incredibly blessed by my family. He has blessed me with strengths in different areas too, and joy in my walk with him. And I feel blessed to have had Nathan as my son, for the short time he was here on this earth. I enjoyed him immensely as a child, and had some good moments with him too as a young man. And I look forward to the time when I will see him again, in glory.

Loving Nathan

EPILOGUE

A few months before Nathan died, I shared in my church fellowship that I was believing for my son to come home to me within three years. I shared that because that is what I felt the Lord had spoken to me. When he came home in a coffin, I did not feel that was the answer to my prayers, or my public declaration.

My prayer for Nathan in the months leading up to his death was that he would come to know that God really loved him. I did not know much about what was happening in his life at the time, but I knew that he left home angry and hurting. I longed for him to come to the realisation that God was for him, despite everything that had happened. Although I believed that Nathan went to be with the Lord, and would have thus come to understand how much he was loved by God, I did not feel this was an answer to my prayers.

I am reminded of a story that I heard many years ago. A man of God, often bringing prophetic words within his ministry in YWAM, gave one such word to a young lady in Hawaii. He informed her that on a certain date, and he gave a specific date, she would meet her bridegroom. The specificity of this prophetic word was unusual even for this man of God, but he had a proven track record of bringing the word of God to people, so this young lady believed him. As the day drew closer, however, she did not focus on improving her looks, but rather she focused on drawing nearer to the Lord whom she served. When the date finally arrived, a friend of hers who had a plane invited her for a flight around the island. She accepted the offer, and the two of them took to the skies. Whilst in the air the plane malfunctioned, and it crashed to the ground, killing both of them.

And so she met her bridegroom, Jesus Christ, the son of God. Sometimes our understanding of death is short-sighted. We think it is to be avoided at all costs, and we do whatever we can to push it further into the future. For those of us who love the Lord, death is the entrance into the presence of God in a way that we have barely tasted here. I am definitely not advocating not taking care of ourselves in order to die sooner, but for those that God calls home, maybe it is a beautiful thing.

Nathan did not finish all that God had for him on this earth. But certainly now he is in a much better place. There is no more torment for him. I am happy for him. I wish to make a few other statements.

Firstly, as I said before, I believe in prayer, and I believe that God has restricted himself to the prayers of believers. An example is found in the book of Acts. In Chapter 12, James, the brother of John, has been killed. The church was taken by surprise but were soon prepared to do spiritual battle when King Herod followed this atrocity up by arresting Peter.

> So Peter was kept in prison, but the church was earnestly praying to God for him. (Acts 12:5)
> The church prayed, and in response to their prayers Peter was rescued from prison by an angel. Then Peter came to himself and said, "Now I know without a doubt that the Lord has sent his angel and rescued me from Herod's clutches and from everything the Jewish people were hoping would happen." (Acts 12:11)

Epilogue

It was not that the Lord cared more about what happened to Peter than to James; I believe it was because he was able to move in response to his people praying. I believe that God hears our cries to him, and he responds to our faith. I do not have the answer as to why God did not bring wholeness to my son, or why he watched him drown. Maybe without my prayers it would have been even harder for Nathan, I do not know. I do know that I need to continue to pray, for myself, my family, my friends, my country, and so much more.

I believe that God loves me. Was my son's death an expression of that love? I cannot answer that. But I know that I am loved by God, and so was Nathan, and so are you. The most important demonstration of God's love is the death of the Lord Jesus, for me as much as for everyone else. The sinless Son of God, dying on a cross, the perfect sacrifice. And because of his death and resurrection you and I are able to come into relationship with God himself. I am forever grateful. I hope you are too.

I believe God's love is also personal and intimate, available to you and I uniquely today for our lives. While I have always been proud of my intellectual abilities, I never saw myself as attractive. I often wondered if I was worthy of love. My parents kept these little score books, and whenever we did something good we got a check mark. I always did better than my brother and sister, partly I think because I wanted to be loved. My parents were good people, but they were not good at showing affection. I never actually felt loved by anyone until I met Mike. Recently the Lord brought a memory back to me, of when I was a little girl rushing home from school, desperate to use the bathroom. When I arrived home, the door was locked, and no one was there to let me in. I ended up peeing myself. A few minutes later my mother arrived home on her bicycle. I am sure she was only a few minutes late, but it was enough time for me to have an embarrassing accident which made me feel that I was not important enough for my mother to come home on time. In that memory, the Lord whispered to me *"Mary, you are loveable."* Somehow I had embraced the lie that I was not loveable, that there was something lacking in me. I intend to fully embrace the truth now that I am indeed loveable, so I speak it out every day. Apparently it takes around 30 days time to change a habit, so that's a good goal. The Lord is so faithful to continue ministering life to me, healing me, making me whole.

 I am forever grateful that Jesus drew me to himself, that he changed me, helped me to accept who I am, helped me to believe that I am lovable, and also that he brought a young man into my life who became my husband. And not only did I receive a husband, but after being told that I would not be able to have children, I gave birth to three of them! My two daughters continue to be a great blessing in my life, and both are seeking to walk with God and to please him.

 And blessing upon blessing, Abigail and Jon have five wonderful children, all of whom I thoroughly enjoy being Granny to! They had not intended to have five, but at the end of Abigail's last pregnancy she gave birth to triplets! With three little ones we would walk in the door, and immediately be told to wash our hands and pick up a baby! I loved it. I still love it. All five of the children bring so much joy to Mike and I.

 I am incredibly blessed too with a home with a swimming pool in the back garden. Though I left England many years ago, this still seems extravagant to me. During the summer there is rarely a day when I do not swim around in circles, praying and giving thanks to the Lord. I am blessed also with a wonderful job. I retired from teaching at school in order to help my daughter with the triplets. I love to teach though, and was quickly able to find a part-time position at the local college. And I have some wonderful friends. Those who stood by me during the death of my son, and many whom I have only met since that time. And thanks to modern communications, I have also been able to connect with so many friends that I left behind in England and the Netherlands, or other places around the world. My pets have been a blessing too, we currently have two cats and a dog. I especially appreciate my dog, since she ensures that I walk at least twice every day. And I am healthy. In fact I am probably healthier now than during most of my life. I am also very privileged to attend two churches, both of which are a great blessing to me. I could continue for many more pages, because I am blessed over and over again by the Lord.

Yes, I have suffered a tragic loss. I am still conscious of that imaginary chain that hangs around my neck and reminds me that Nathan is no longer with us. Other things remind me too, like when the son of a friend gets married. I rejoice with them, yet I am sad inside because I will never attend the marriage of my son. And when a friend receives a new grandchild through their son, I am reminded again that Nathan will never give me grandchildren. I will not deny those moments of sadness, nor will I pretend that they do not still sometimes happen. But I will not dwell on those moments. I choose to quickly focus on what I have, rather than what I do not have. And the more I choose to do that the easier it becomes. I can declare that God is good, and I truly do believe it.

Loving Nathan

APPENDIX: REFLECTIONS ON HEAVEN & HELL

Who goes to Heaven and who goes to Hell? That is not an easy question for anyone to answer. I once heard a joke about someone who died and went to Heaven. St. Peter walks him quietly past a large group of people, asking him not to make any noise. Later, when the person asks St. Peter why that was necessary, Peter replies *"They are the Baptists, and they think that they are the only ones here."* You could probably change Baptists for many other groups too.

    Several years ago, as part of my Masters of Divinity degree, I did a lot of research on hell. I read several different perspectives, from the belief that anyone who has not asked Jesus to be the Lord of their life goes to hell, to the understanding that no one goes to hell except demons, and even the belief that hell does not exist at all. I read all the various Scriptures used to defend every viewpoint. My professor was very supportive, and would suggest further readings backing up each different thought. Then I put it all together into an essay and submitted it for evaluation. Before reading it, my professor asked me what my own conclusions were. I had come to believe that God did not send humans to eternal damnation. Not that everyone went to heaven either, but that those who chose to reject God and his love for them would simply sleep forever. After I had reached my conclusions he informed me that after much prayer and study, his father had come to the same belief, and had been shunned by his community as a result.

I am encouraged to be living in an age when we are given the privilege to think and hear from God for ourselves. I became a Christian when I was seventeen and at that time I simply accepted everything that my pastor and elders taught me. I am much older now and after many years of sorting through what I was taught I still fully embrace the truth that Jesus, the Son of God, lived on this earth and died for my sins and the sins of the whole world. On the third day he was resurrected, and he now continues alive, interceding for us. I have thrown a few other things away, however. I certainly do not have everything sorted out yet. Another of my professors at Seminary laughingly informed us that there often comes a time when we think we have the whole jigsaw of our faith sorted out. We know exactly what we believe, and have our theology totally figured out. Then we look to the side of our completed puzzle and recognise that there are a few pieces still lying there, not a part of the finished picture.

We should always be learning, always asking questions of God and of the Scriptures. That, I believe, is very healthy.

The biggest question that I have about the traditional evangelical understanding of hell, as a lifelong committed Christian, is the same question that the world has. How could an eternally loving, merciful, kind God, send a young man of twenty-four, who got drunk over the holiday weekend, dived into the lake and then drowned, to an eternity of torment? Depending on your idea of when someone becomes an adult, he would have had at the most, ten years that he was not a child. He may have had one or two Christian influences in his life, and he may have responded arrogantly and selfishly. He made some stupid choices. He did not choose to follow God, if perhaps he had any idea that God wanted him to follow him. So after that short time, he is now going to be punished for all of endless eternity? That really is not the picture of God I get from reading the Bible. I'm not talking about Nathan specifically here, just a hypothetical young man.

    I would like to point out that I firmly believe Scripture gets the last word. I love God's written word, and I have read it nearly every day for over forty-five years. I have read the whole Bible over twenty times, and the New Testament perhaps a hundred times. And each time I read it God speaks to me through it. There is simply no book like it. It is alive with truth. That being said, the only Scripture that I found to speak clearly of people being tormented after they die is in a parable. A parable that many theologians say is not about hell at all but about the rich needing to help the poor (Luke 16:19-31). Nowhere else in Scripture is there an indication that people who fail to choose to follow God in their lifetime will find themselves in eternal, conscious torment.

    The two Scriptures that are most often used to argue eternal punishment are Matthew 25:46 and 2 Thessalonians 1:7b-9. In Matthew we read *"Then they will go away to eternal punishment, but the righteous to eternal life."* This is the only place in Scripture that mentions eternal punishment. When reading ancient literature, we have to ask what these words would have meant to those who wrote them and to those who read them. When we read the word 'eternal' today, we think of time that goes on forever, but this is not what the original readers would have understood it to mean. For them, this language concerns the age to come, and Christians are invited to begin to experience the new reality now (1 John 5:11). The words translated as *eternal punishment* would mean punishment in the age to come as opposed to the present age. Eternal life is primarily a quality of life, not a duration of life. Thus Matthew is not speaking of punishment without end, it is speaking of punishment in the next age. In 2 Thessalonians we read, "This will happen when the Lord Jesus is revealed from heaven in blazing fire with his powerful angels. He will punish those who do not know God and do not obey the gospel of our Lord Jesus. They will be punished with everlasting destruction and shut out from the presence of the Lord and from the glory of his might."

The punishment that God gives is eternal destruction, not everlasting torment. We can follow this thread in the book of Jude:

> "In a similar way, Sodom and Gomorrah and the surrounding towns gave themselves up to sexual immorality and perversion. They serve as an example of those who suffer the punishment of eternal fire." (Jude 1:7)

The destruction of Sodom and Gomorrah did not last forever, it was a one-time event, and then they were gone. Eternal fire is not fire everlasting, it is fire from a different realm, the realm of the eternal one.

The other Scripture that is often quoted to back up the idea of hell being punishment that goes on forever is Revelation 20:10:

> "And the devil, who deceived them, was thrown into the lake of burning sulfur, where the beast and the false prophet had been thrown. They will be

Appendix: Reflections on Heaven & Hell

tormented day and night forever."

Clearly this is referring not to people, but to the devil, the beast and the false prophet.

I do not believe in hell as eternal conscious torment because the Bible does not teach it. I am not arguing against the Scriptures. I love the Bible and I continue to read it, study it and meditate through it. Just as the Scriptures speak clearly of God's love, they also speak clearly of our need to reach out to the lost and hurting world and share that love with them. This is the great commission that Jesus gives to us, and is the work of every Christian.

When I was a young Christian I once had a very clear dream. In the dream, my mother died, and because she was not in a relationship with the Lord, she went to hell. Then she came back to tell me about it. All she said was, *"The problem with that place is that nobody cares about you."* That was all that she needed to say, because it broke my heart. The thought of my mother, who had sacrificed so much for her family, being in a place where nobody cared about her devastated me. It caused me to go to prayer for her again and again, and gently share the love of the Lord with her. Over the years she responded to that love, and eventually started attending her Anglican church much more frequently (not just at Easter and Christmas). She asked the Lord Jesus to save her, and help her to please him, more than once. God used that simple idea of hell for me, to motivate me to reach out more to my mother, and to pray for her more frequently.

Hell was created for the fallen angels, not for fallen mankind. God's heart towards people is always love. I have read several testimonies of people who persecuted Christians, tortured them, even killed some, and when they cry out to God, he accepts them. Paul from the Bible is one such example, but there are many today, especially in the Muslim world, and also the Communist world. That is the kind of God we serve, one who will receive anyone who cries out to him for help. Anyone.

Scripture is also clear that while Jesus died for the sins of the world, it does not guarantee that everyone will embrace the forgiveness offered to them. We are given the responsibility of sharing the love of God, and people are left with the choice of whether to accept it or not.

When my time comes to die, I really hope that God will be able to say to me, "*Well done, good and faithful servant."* I have previously mentioned my sensing of Nathan crying when he came into the presence of God, because he had failed to live the life that he should have done. Tears of regret, but not tears of rejection. When I die, I want to have no regrets. I want God to be pleased with me.

Nathan left his journals behind when he travelled across Canada to BC. I did not read them while he was still alive, in fact I am not sure I was even aware that they were in our garage, along with so much of his other stuff. But once he had died I knew that I needed to go through all the stuff that I had packed up from his apartment when he was being evicted, and decide what to keep and what to throw out. It was then that I came across his journals. As I read through them I encountered a young man desperately wanting to follow the Lord, but not understanding why others were not seeing his true heart. He obviously struggled to read social cues that others would send his way, and so he would not back off a relationship until it exploded.

Although relationships confused Nathan, he desired very much to please God. There were many of his prayers, and he had written out some Scriptures that helped him. Nathan wanted to follow God for most of his young life. I believe that God welcomed him into heaven, despite the fact that at the time of his death he was rejecting much of what he had previously embraced. God is merciful and I do believe that he gave Nathan the opportunity to repent.

A pastor's wife shared a dream with me once, a vision even, where she saw Nathan in heaven. It was easy for me, when she first shared it, to think that she just wanted to be kind to me and made it up, but over time I have come to accept that yes, she did actually experience seeing Nathan in the presence of God. I hold on to this hope.

www.ingramcontent.com/pod-product-compliance
Lightning Source LLC
Chambersburg PA
CBHW070913080526
44589CB00013B/1283